BETWIXT THE GARDEN: ADULT COLORING BOOK

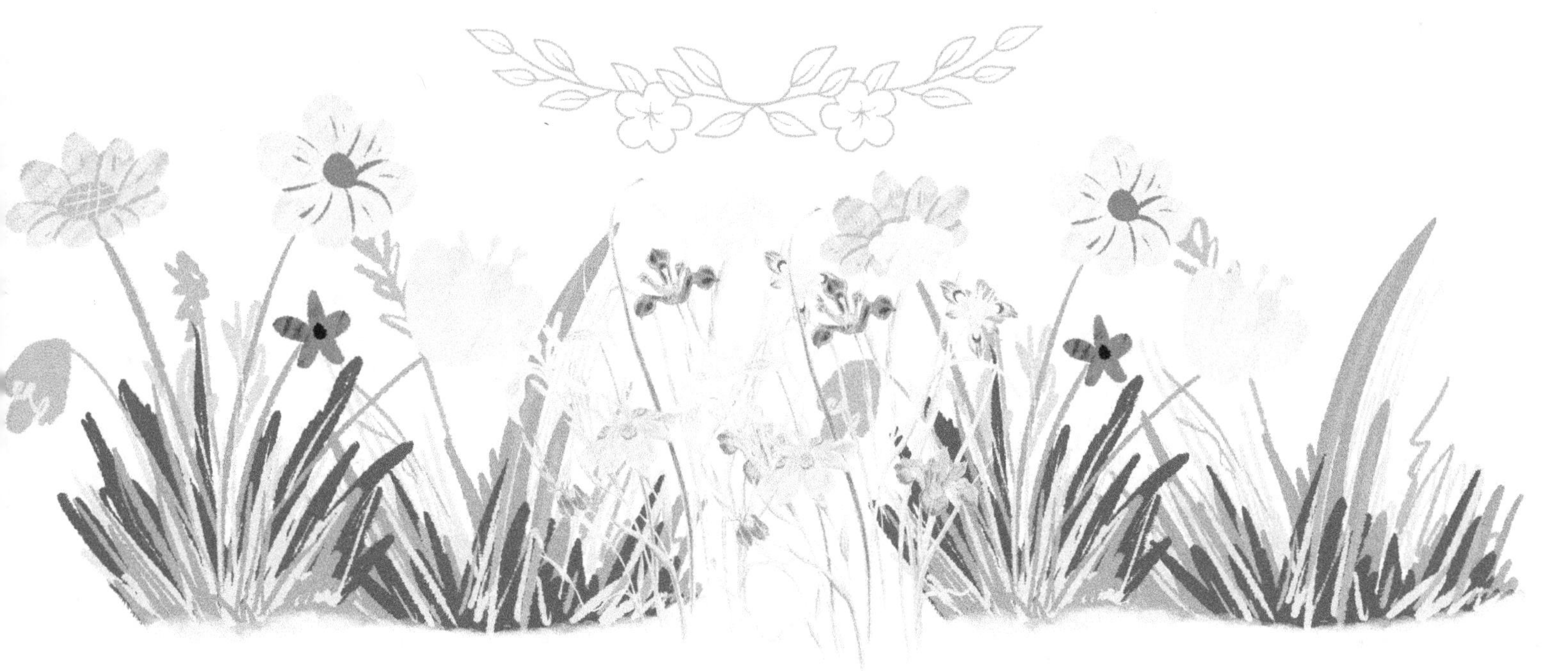

HEARTS OF GOLD

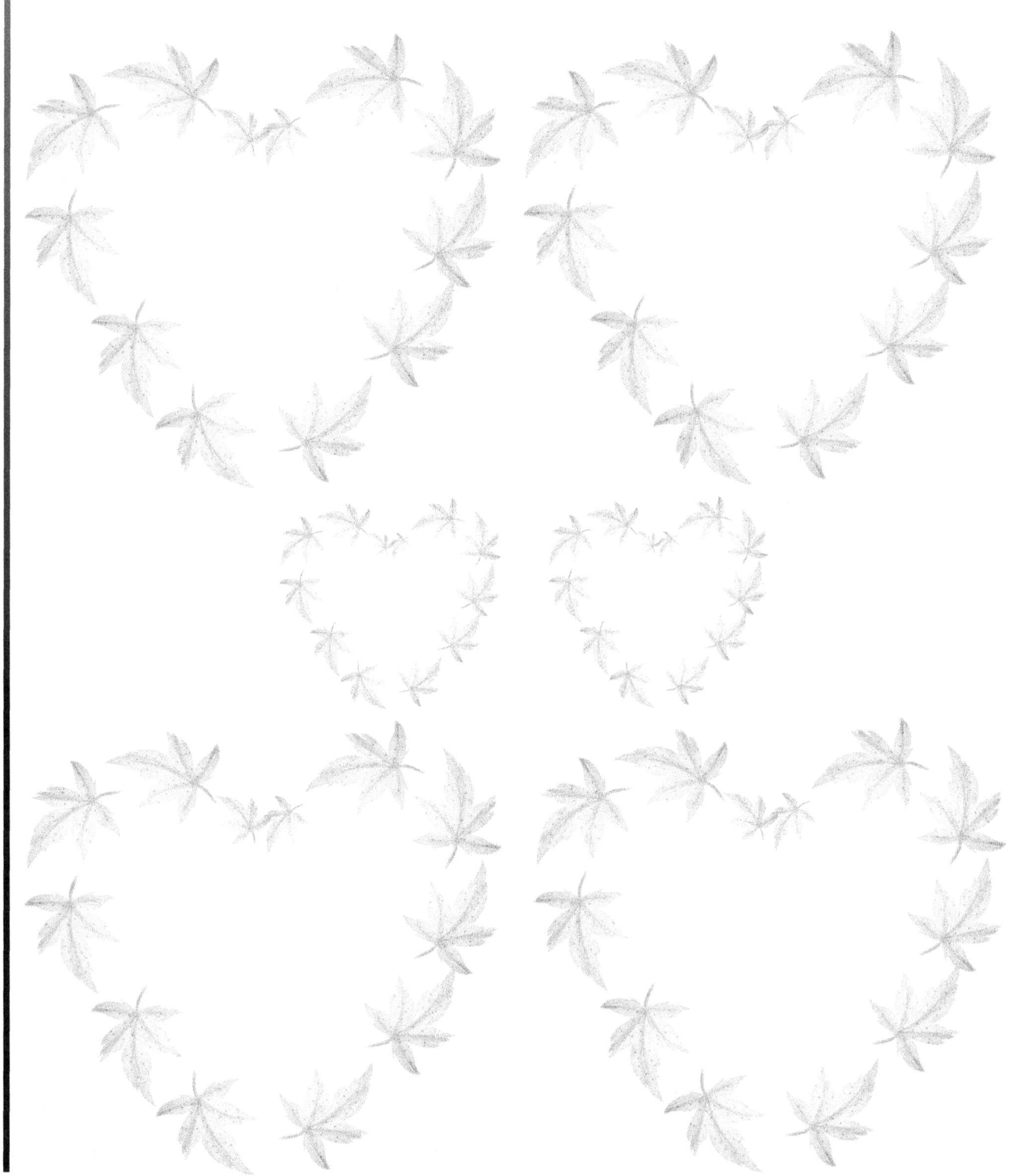

PRETTY FLOWERS

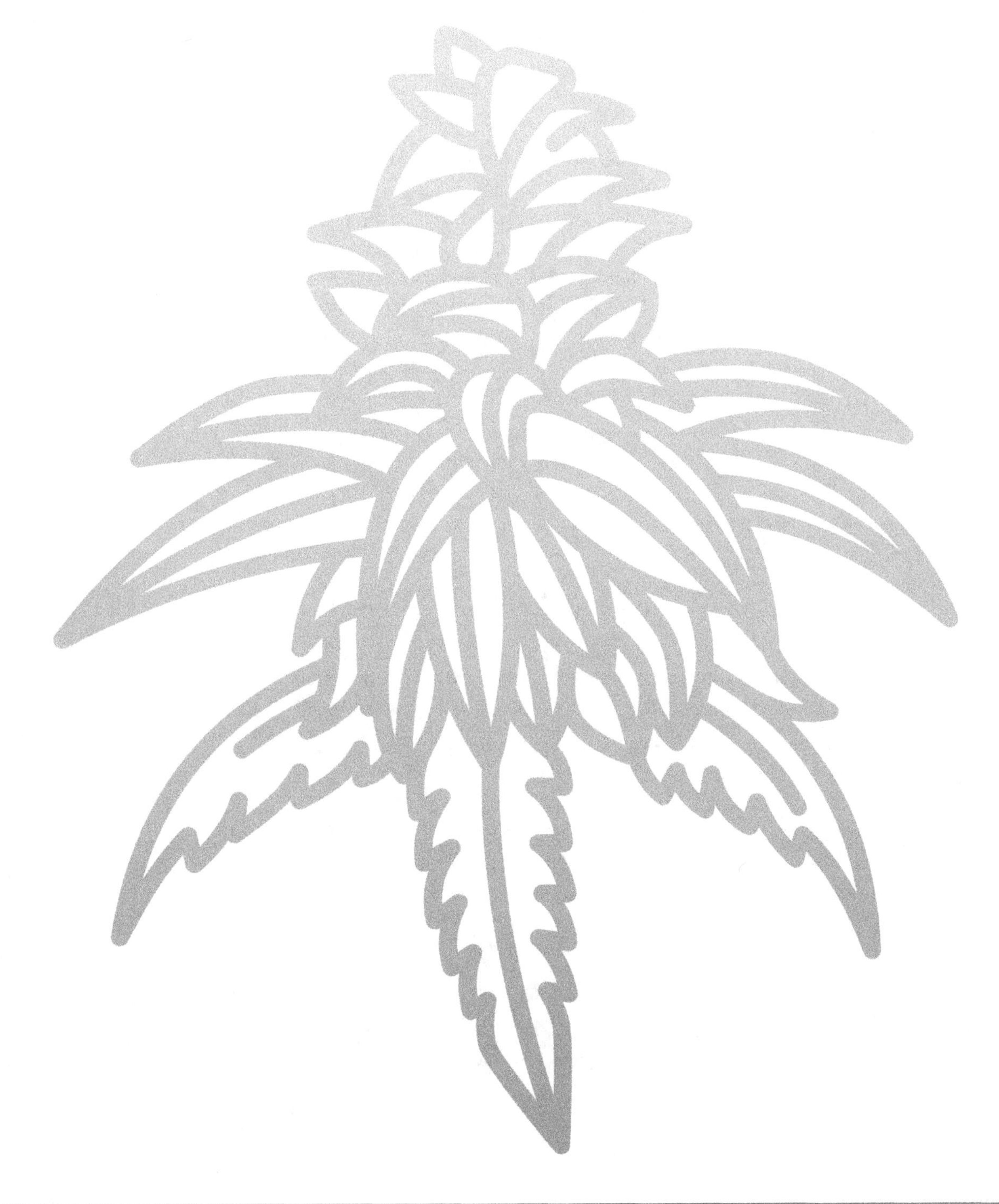

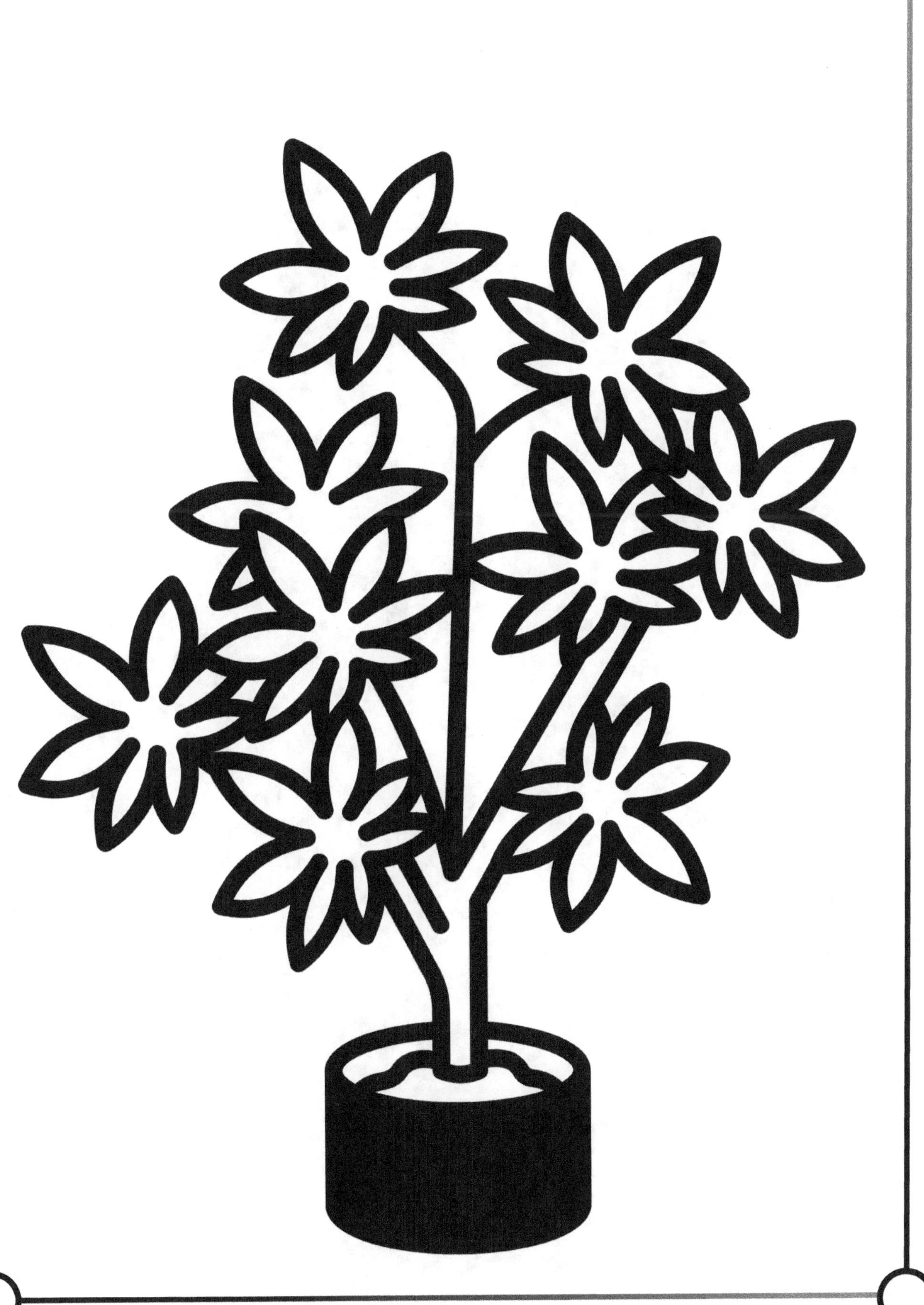

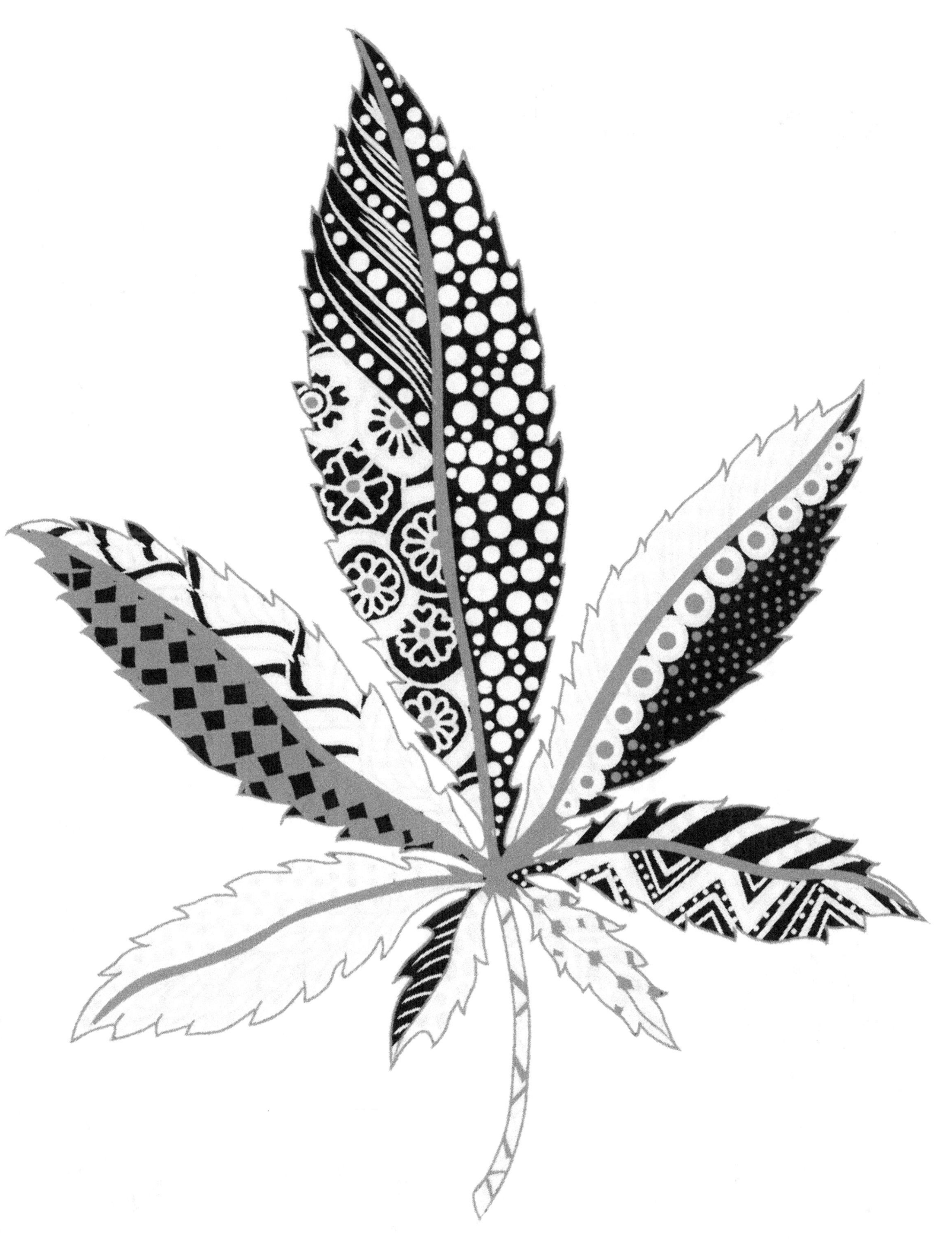

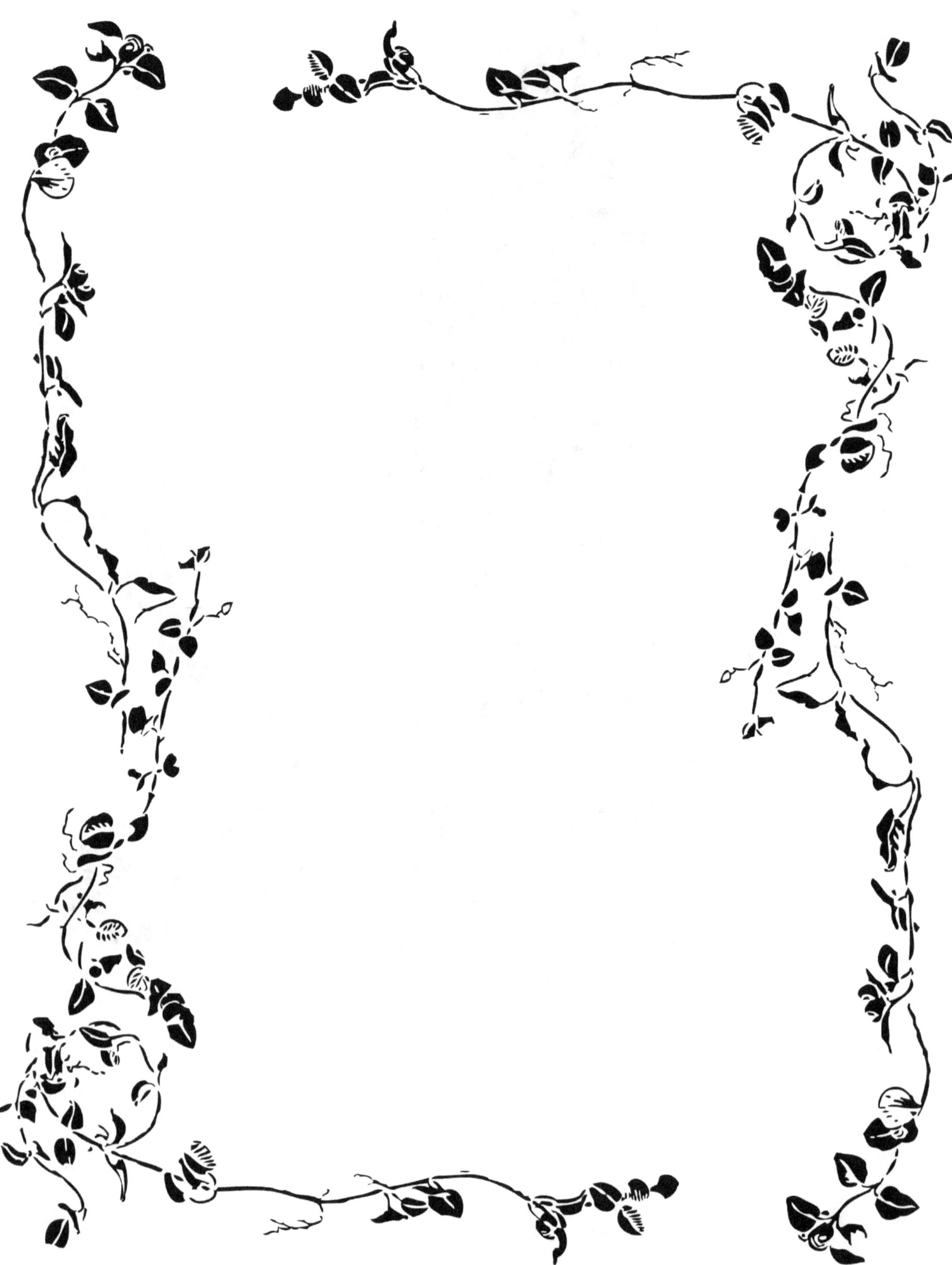

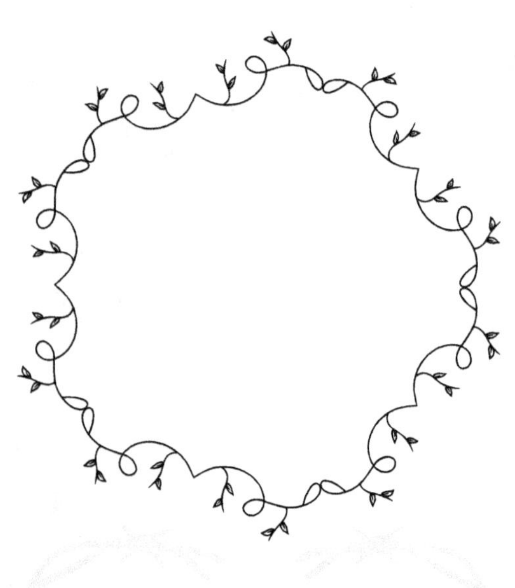

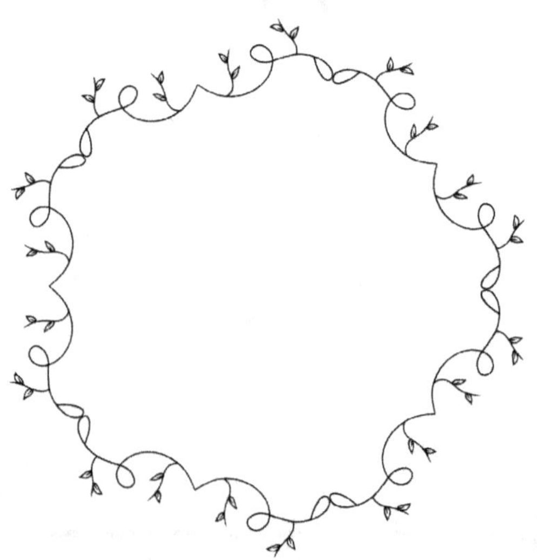

PSYCHEDELICS

LET'S GROW TOGETHER!

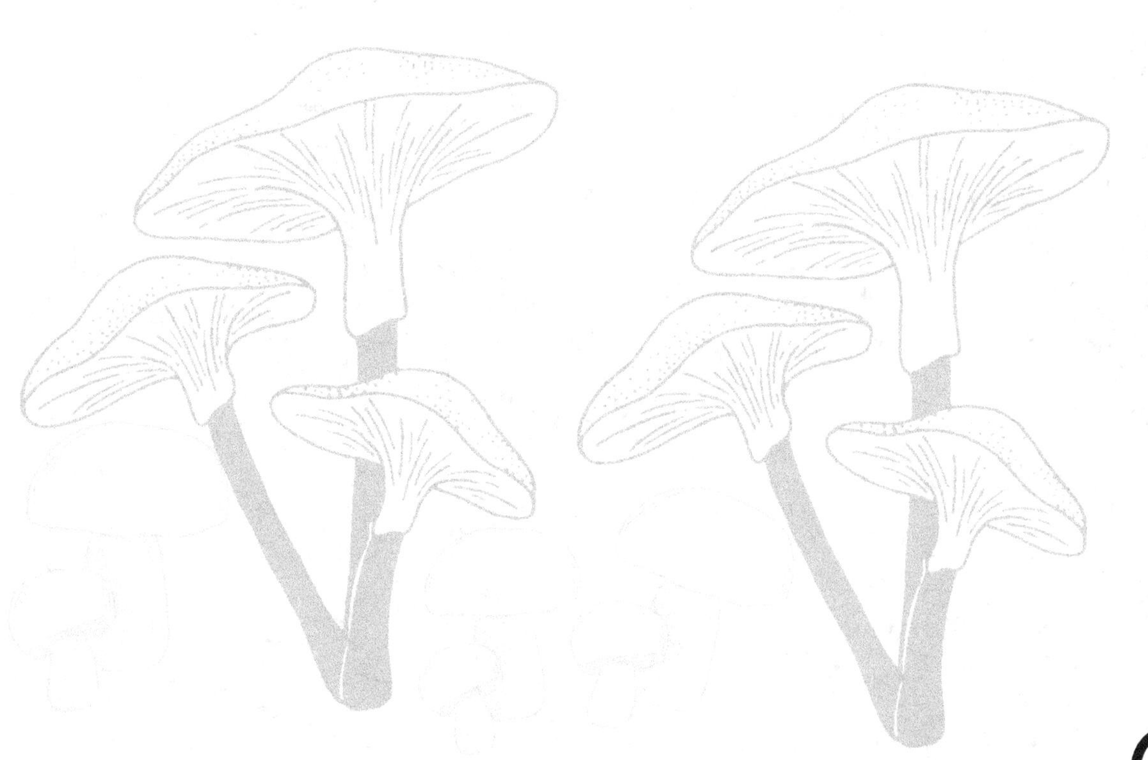

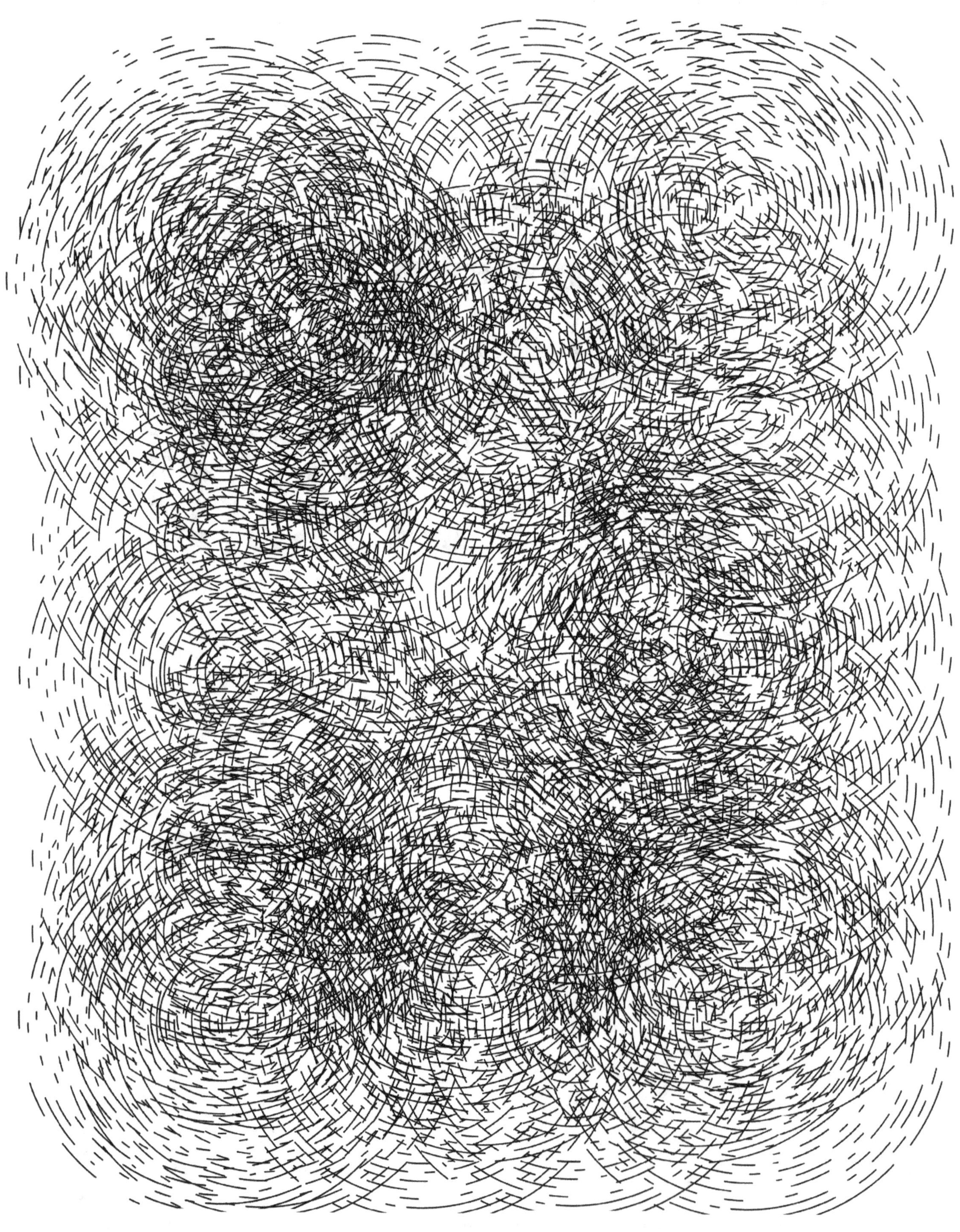

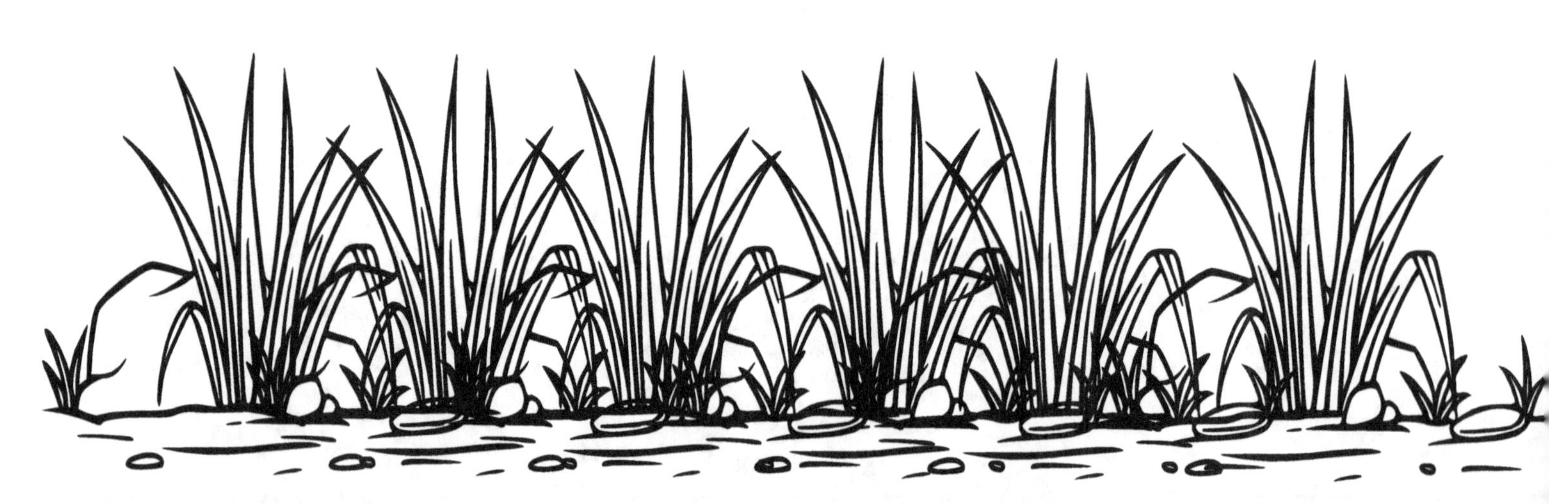

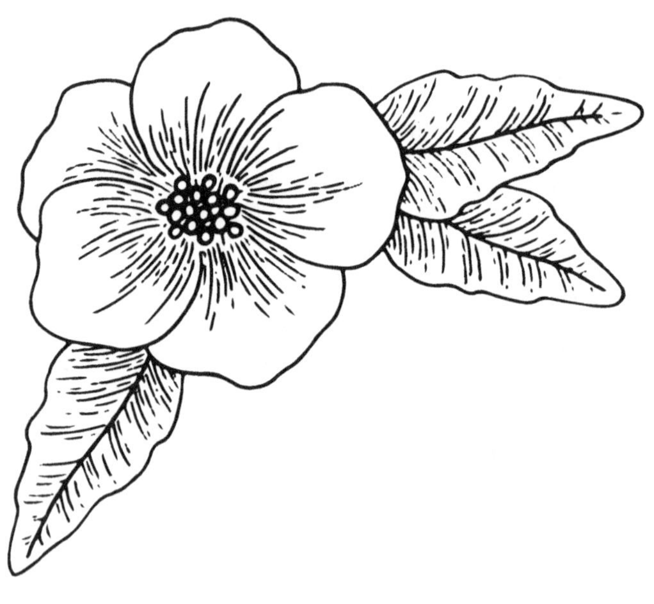
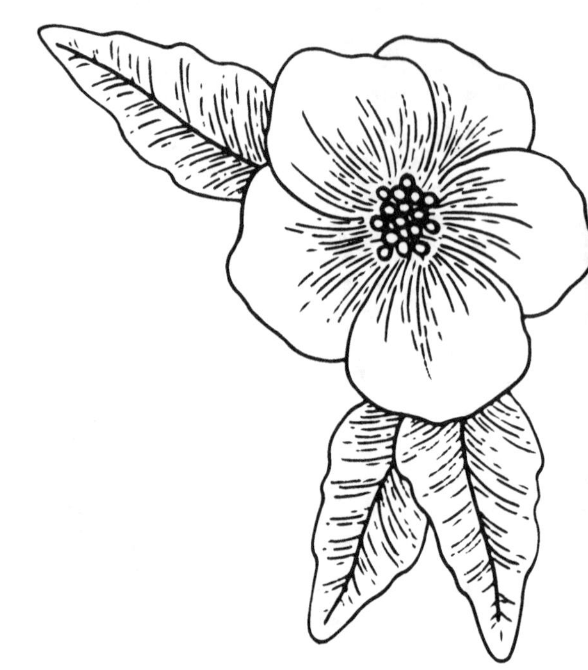
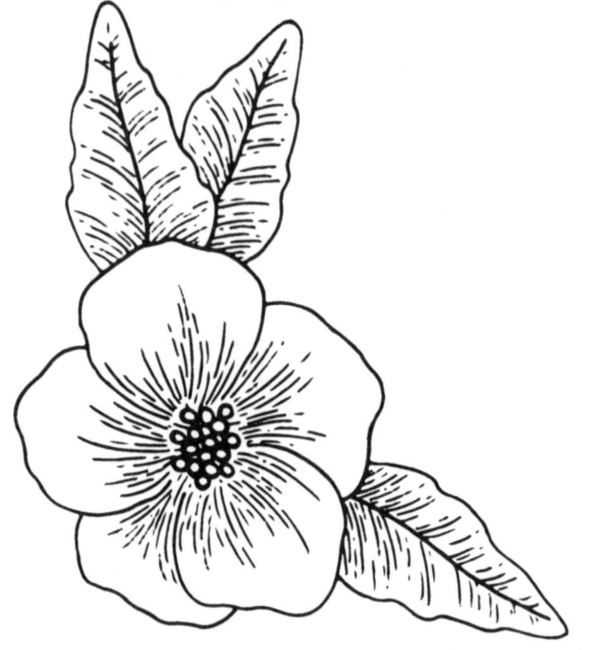
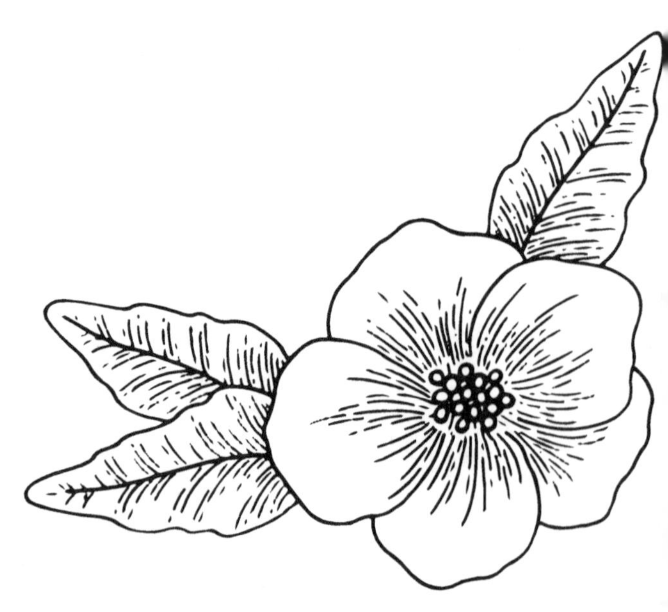

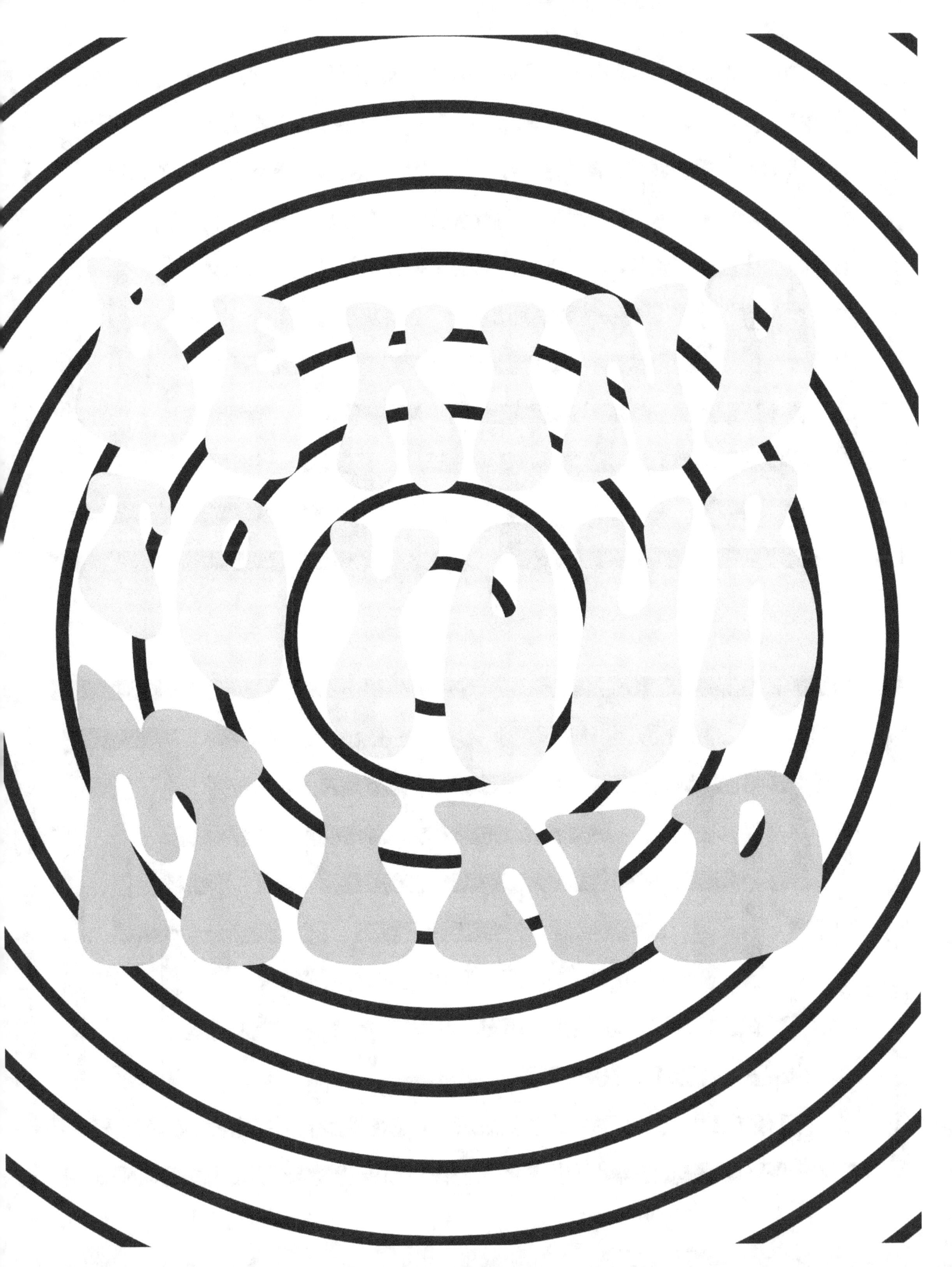

BLOW YOUR MIND

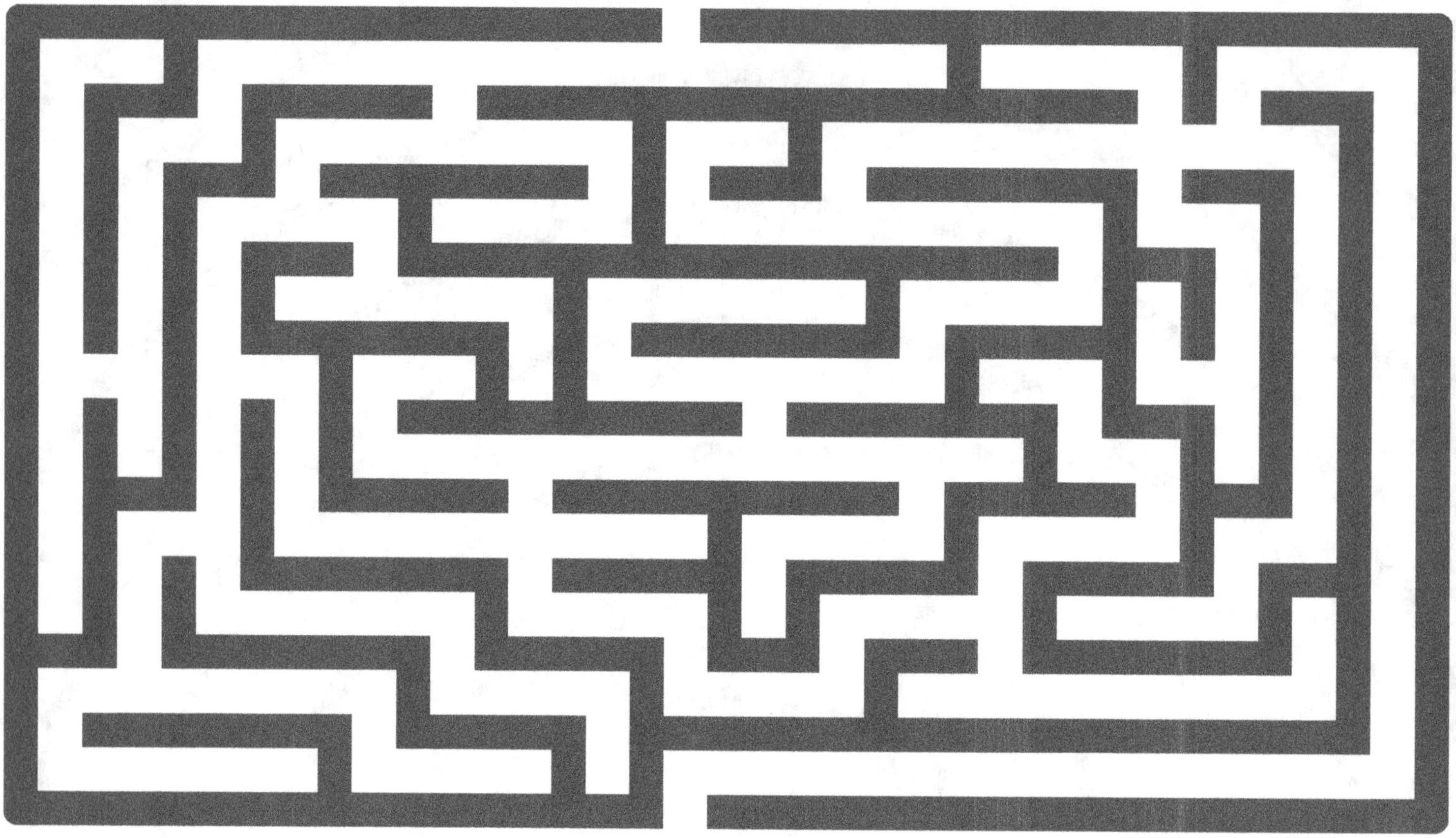

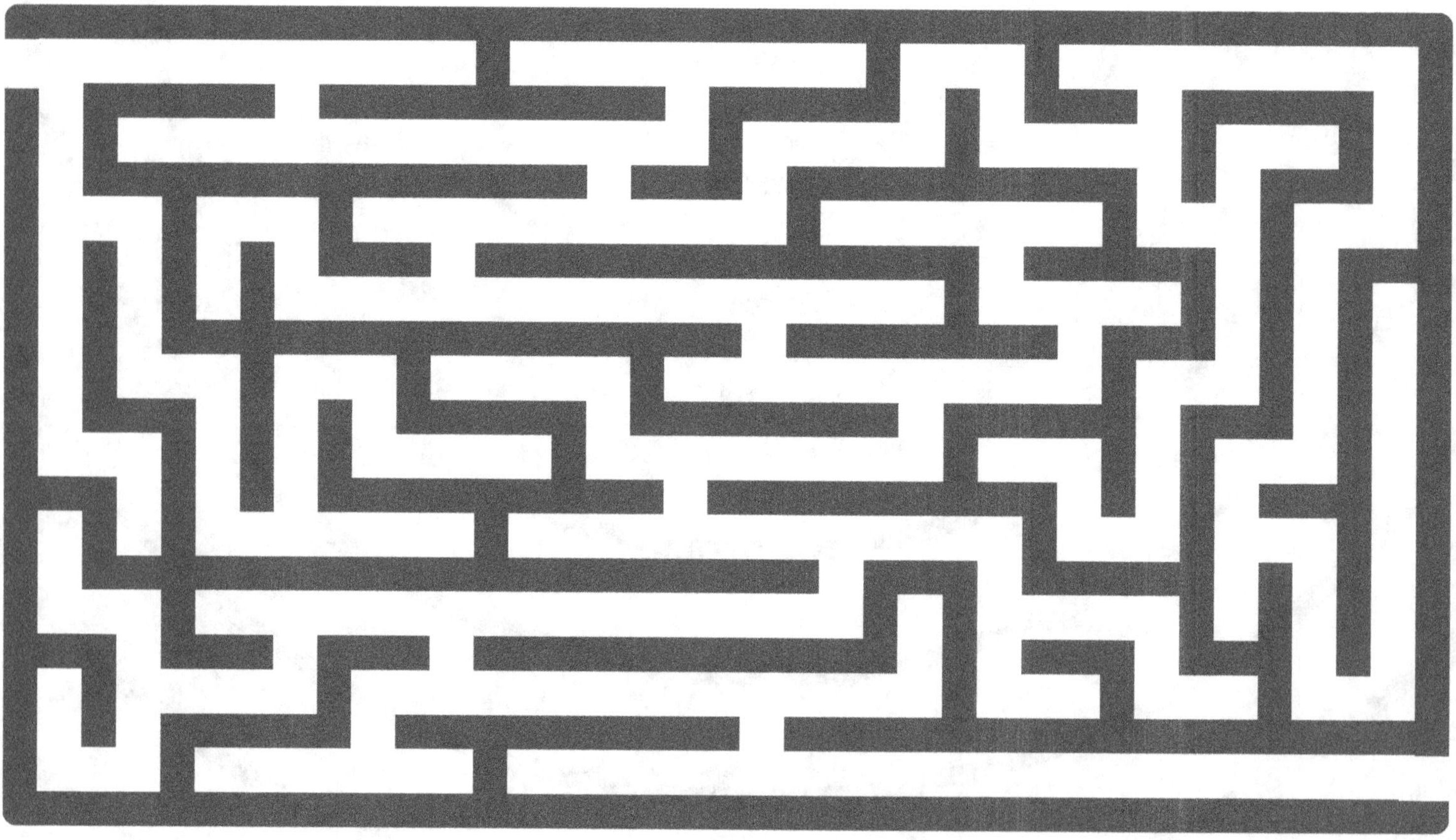

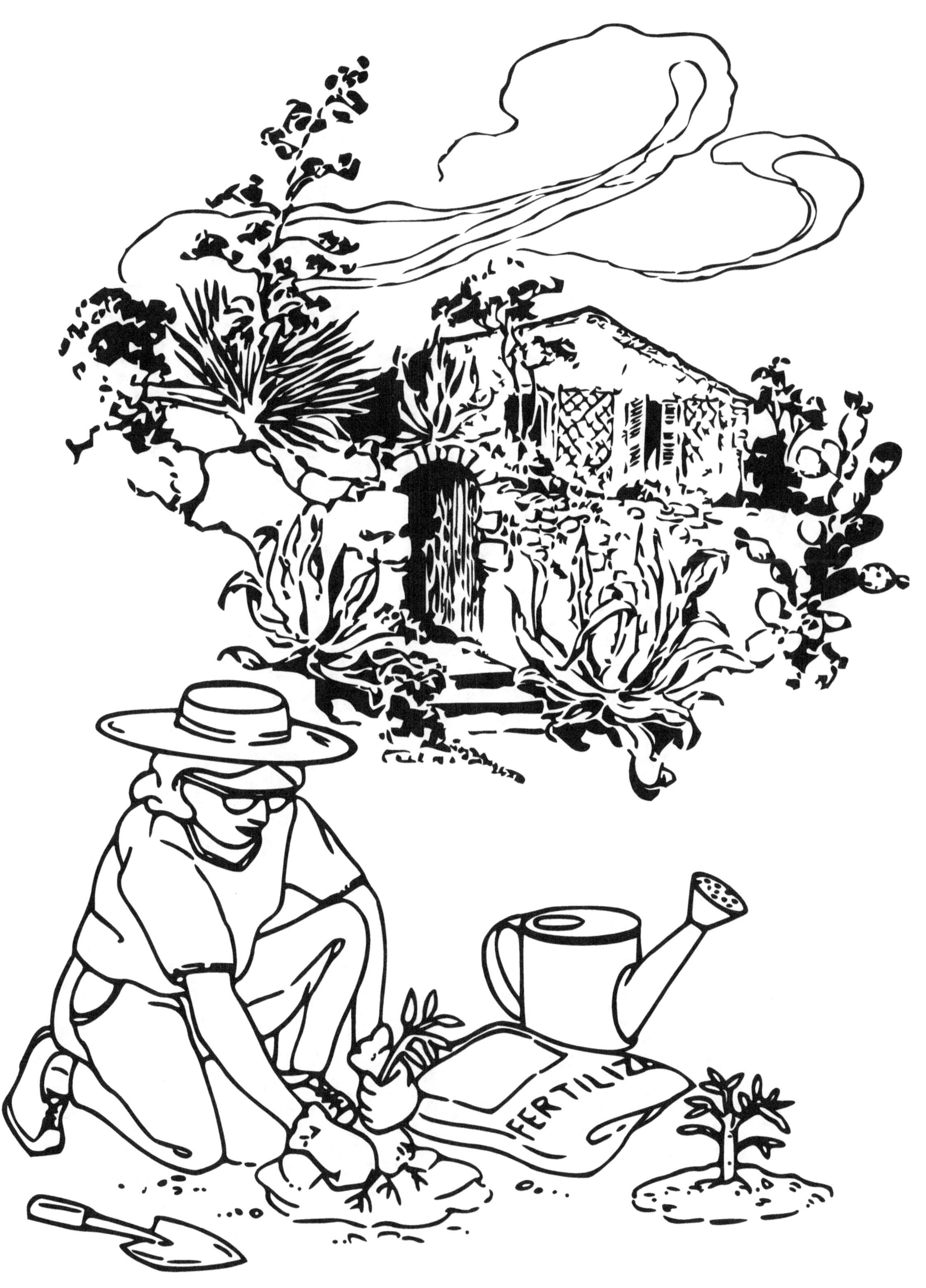

FERTILIZ

MAKE
ROOM FOR
YOURSELF

GARDEN DAZE

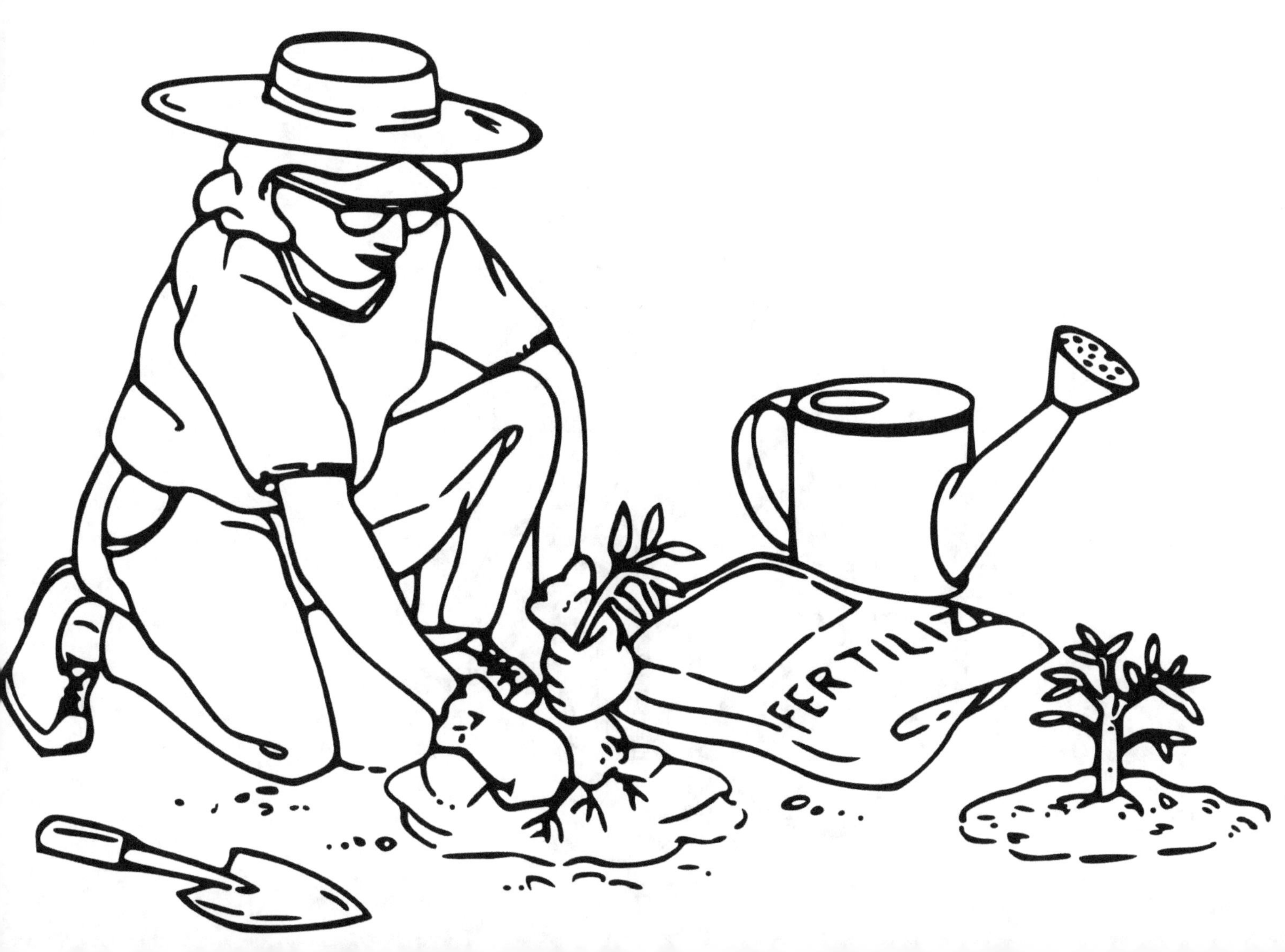

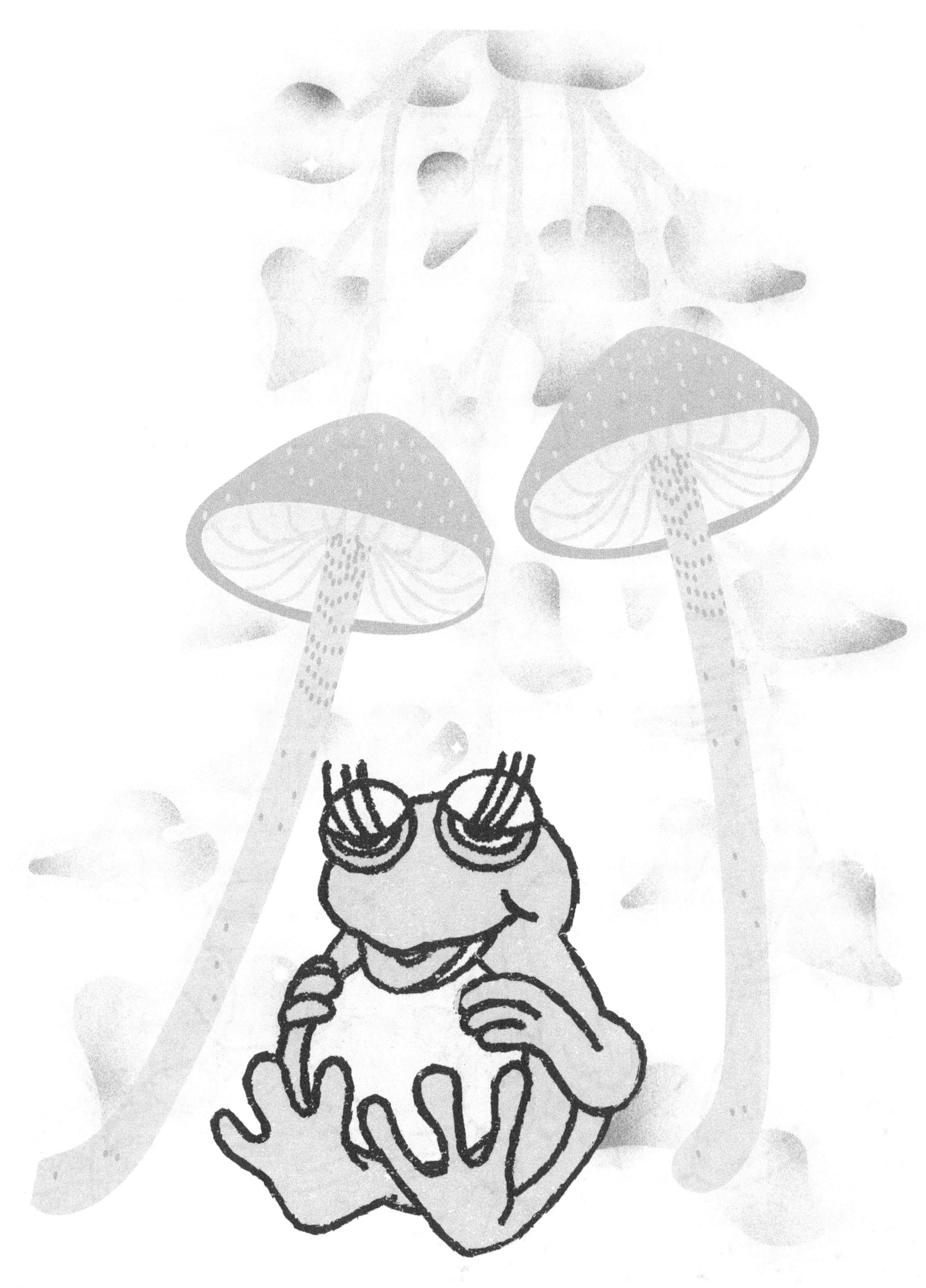

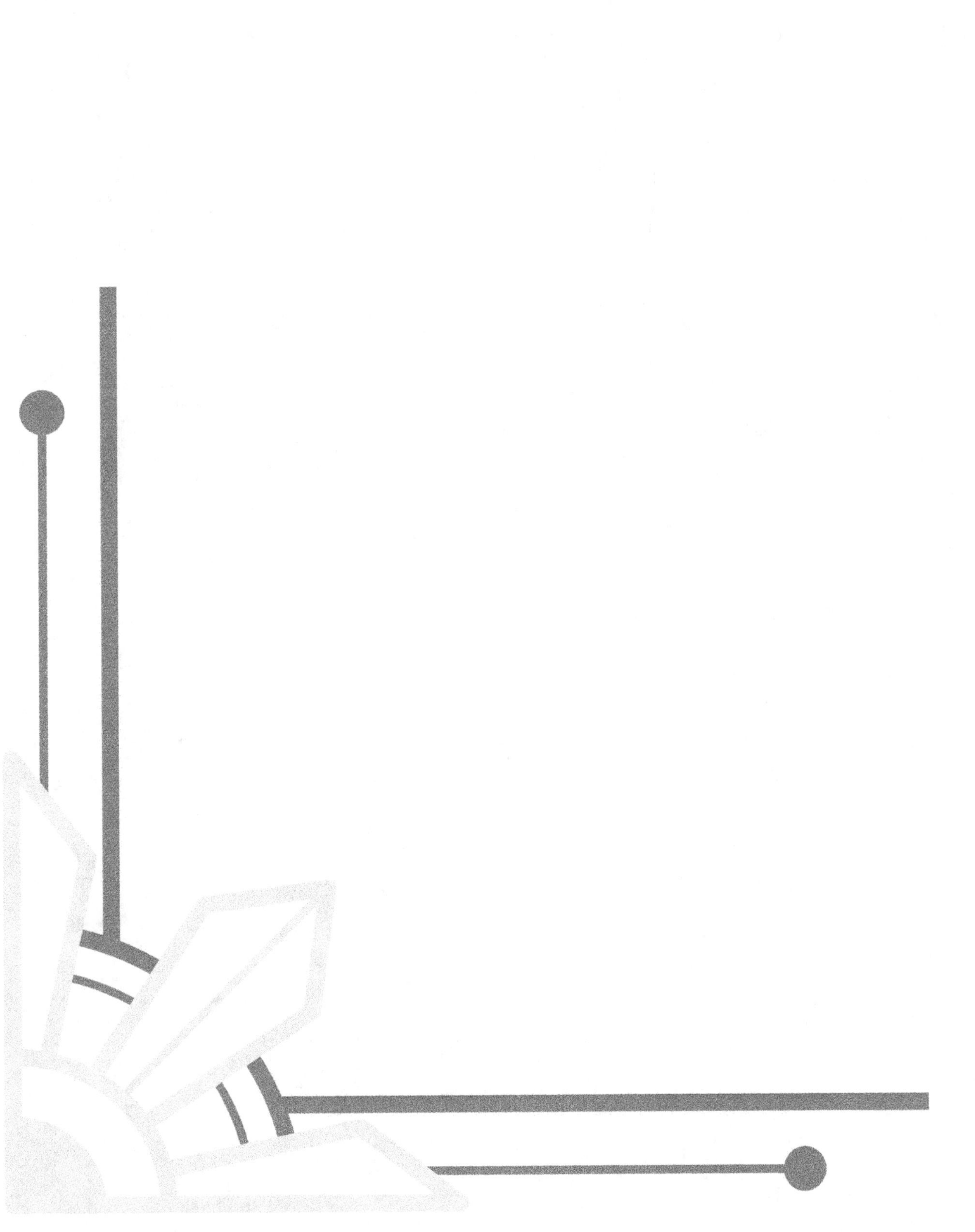

TRUST
YOUR
VISION

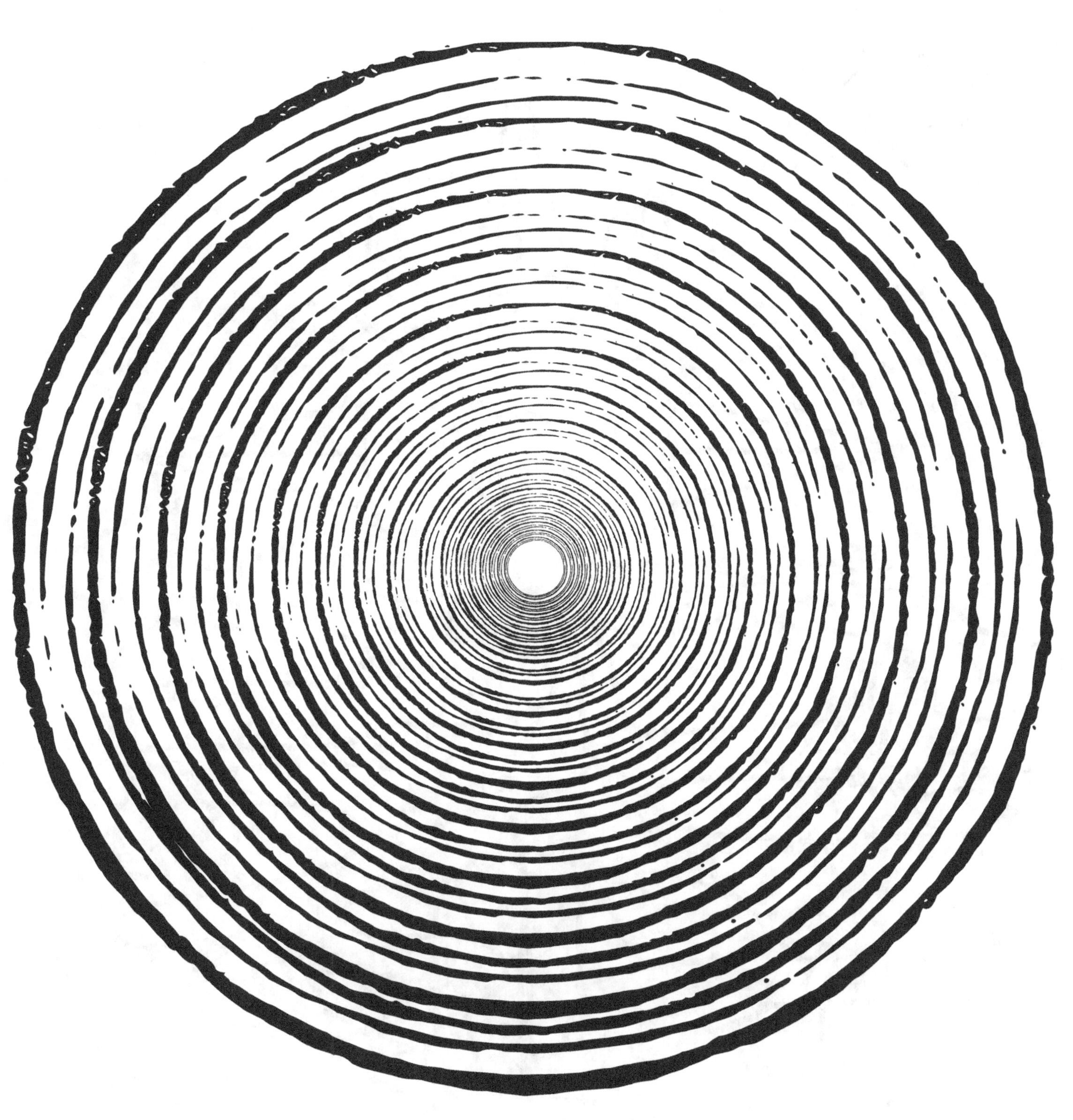

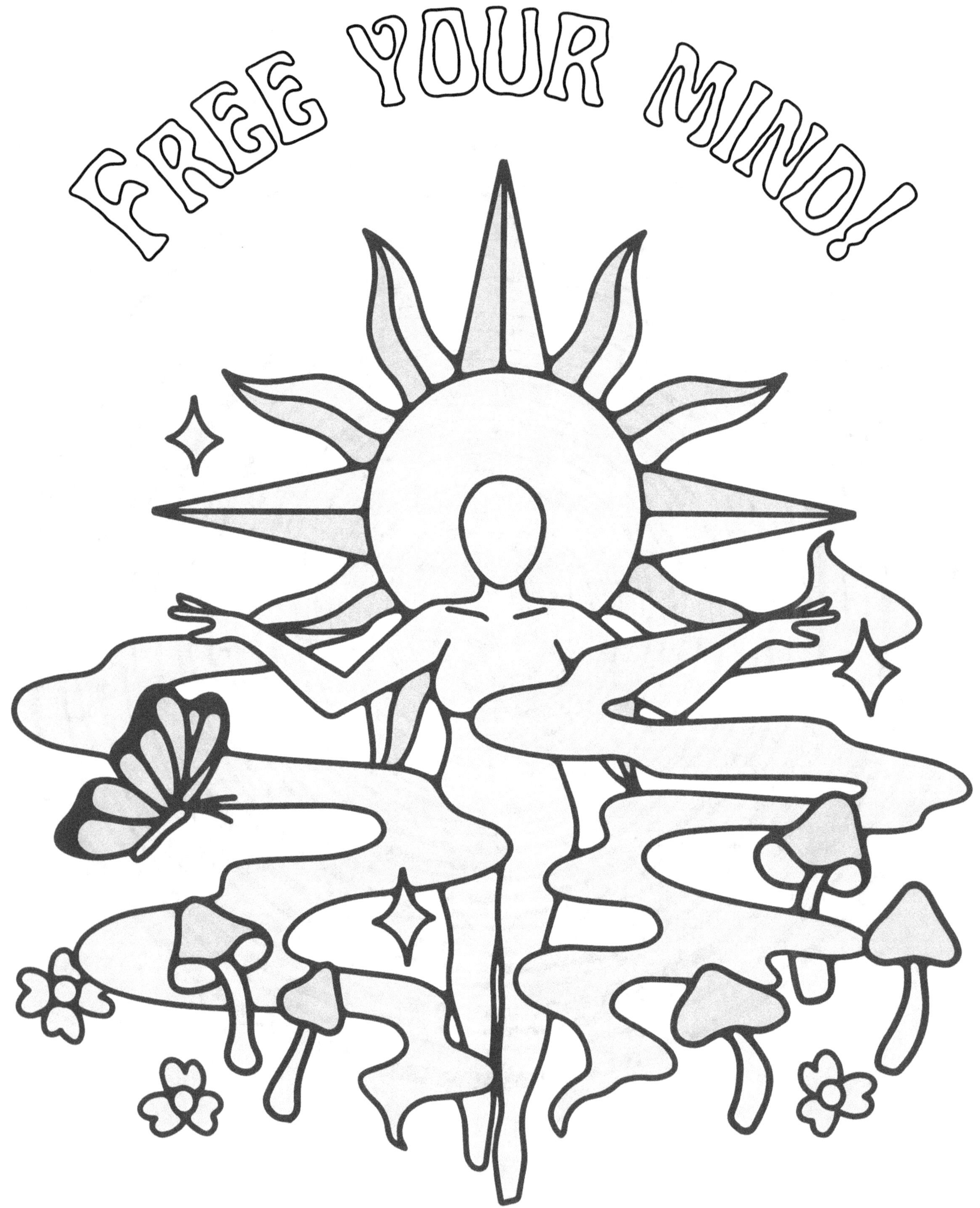
FREE YOUR MIND!

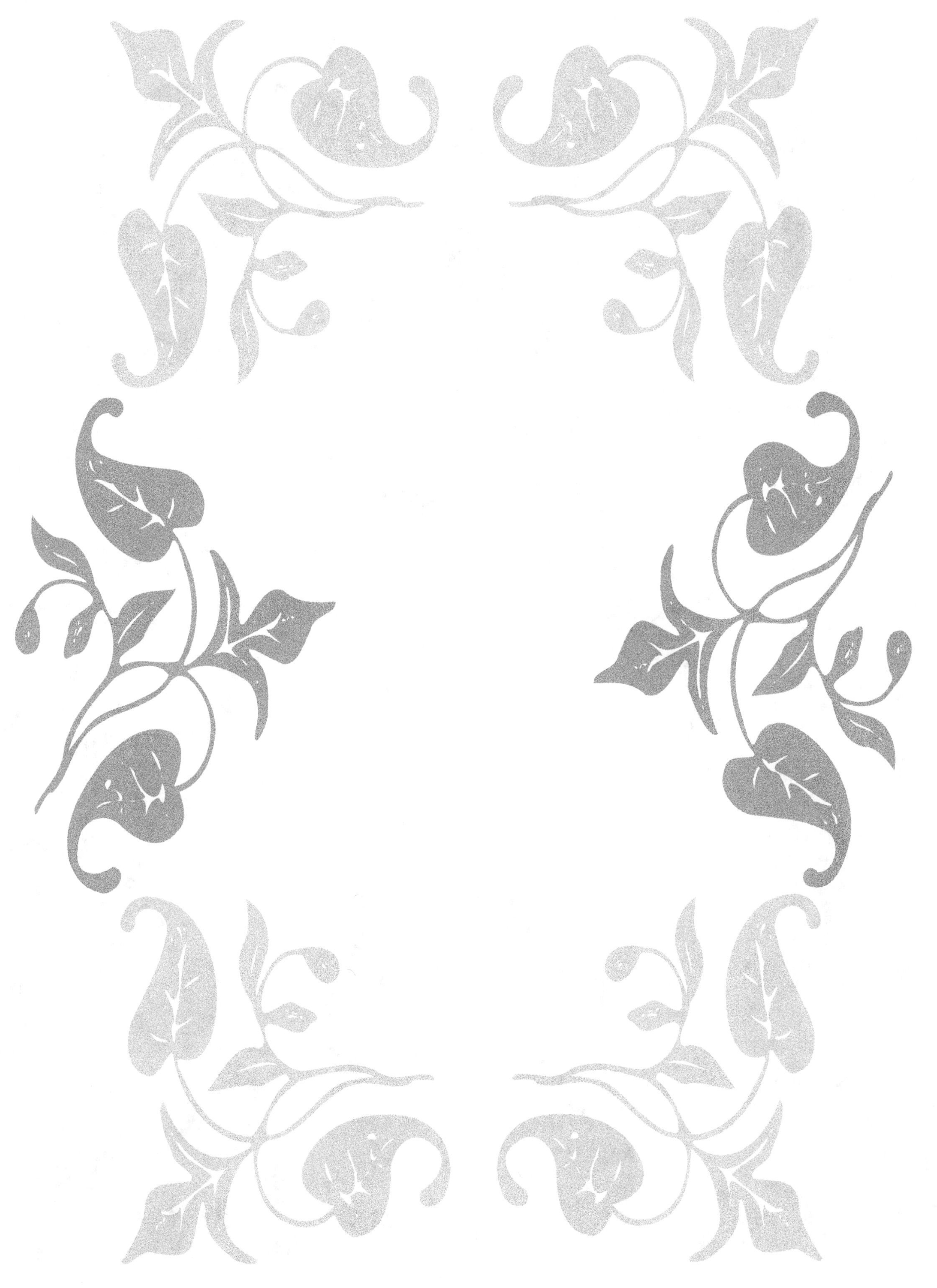

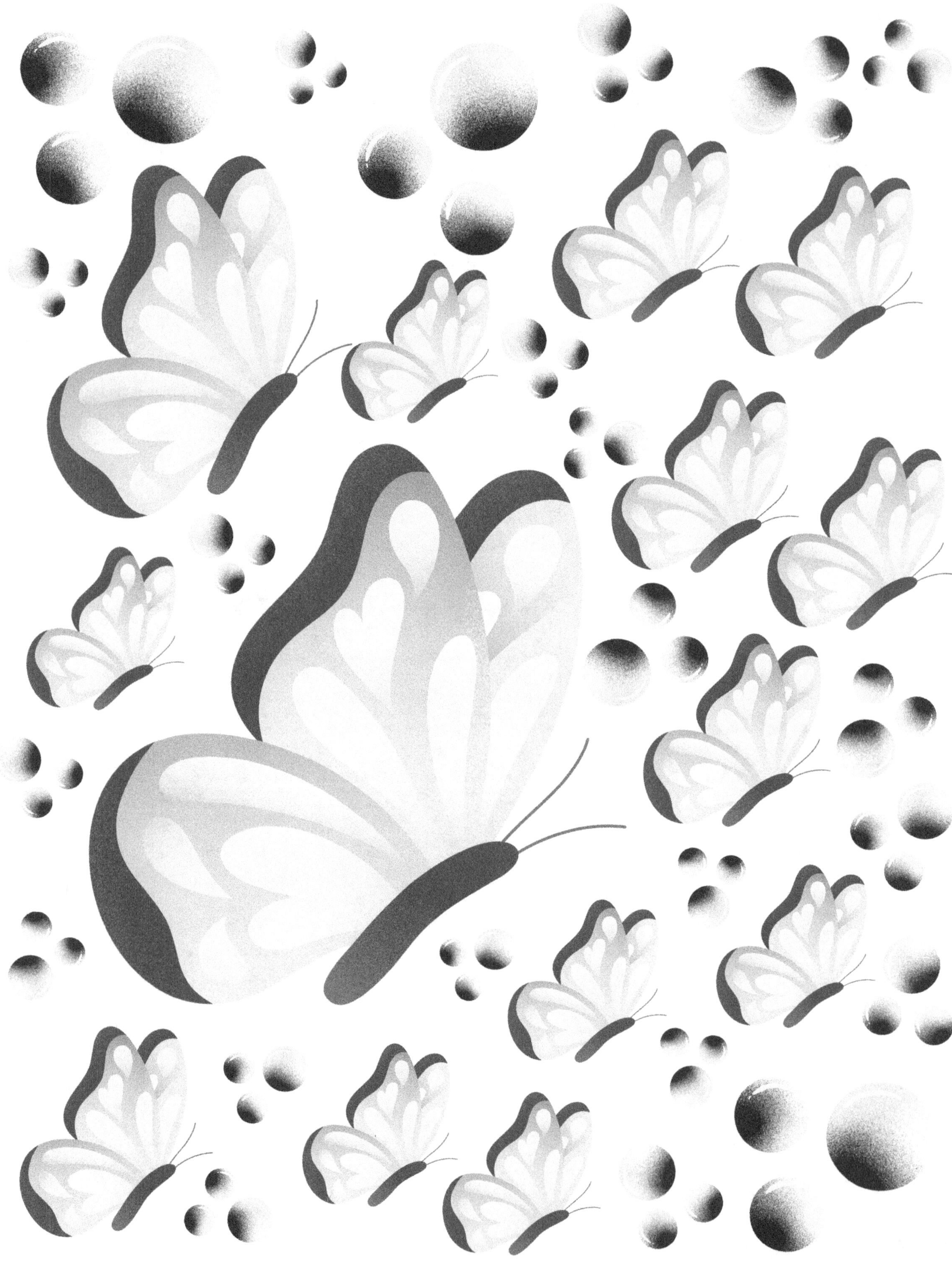

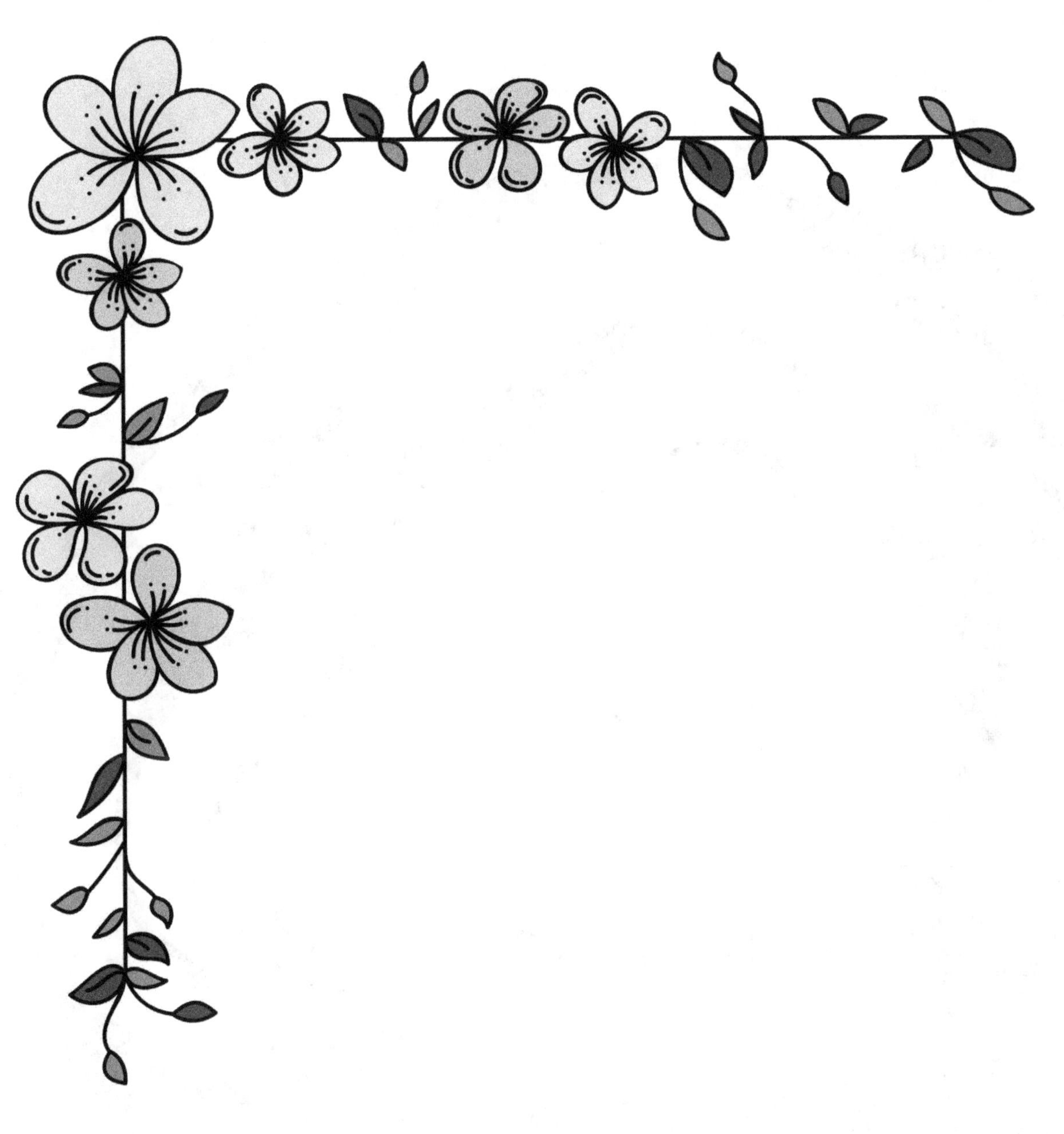

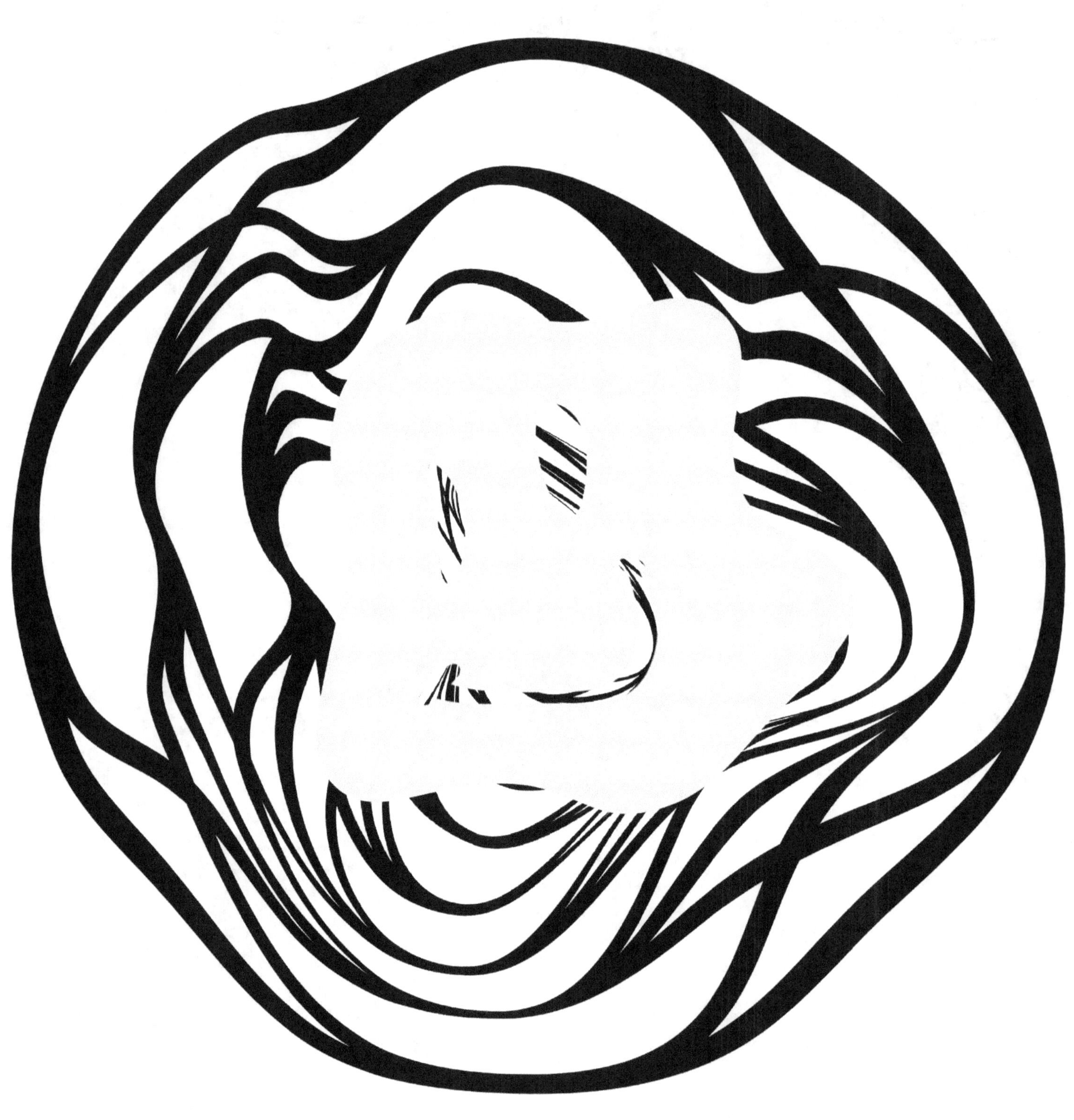

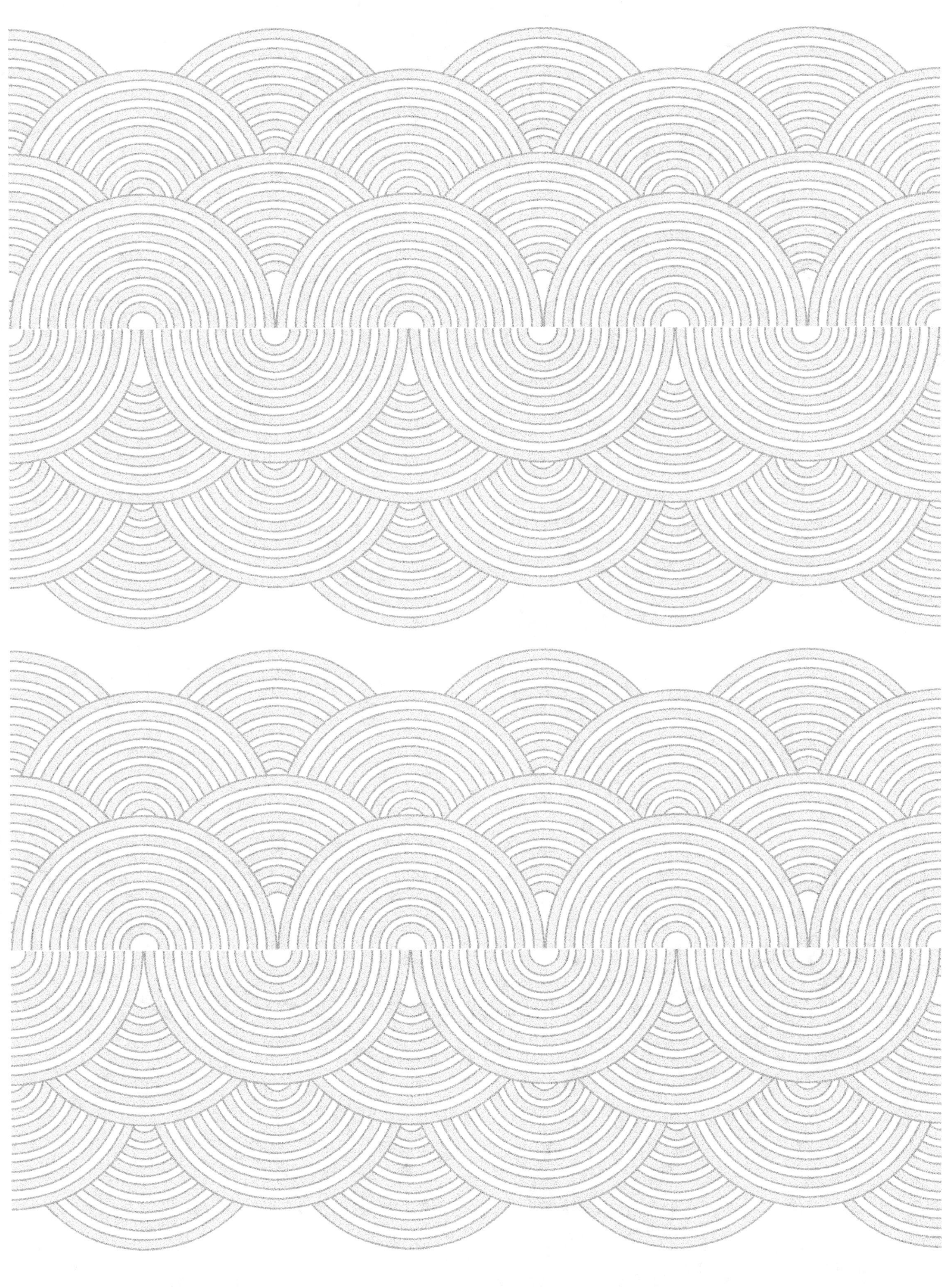

HANGING WITH PLUTO

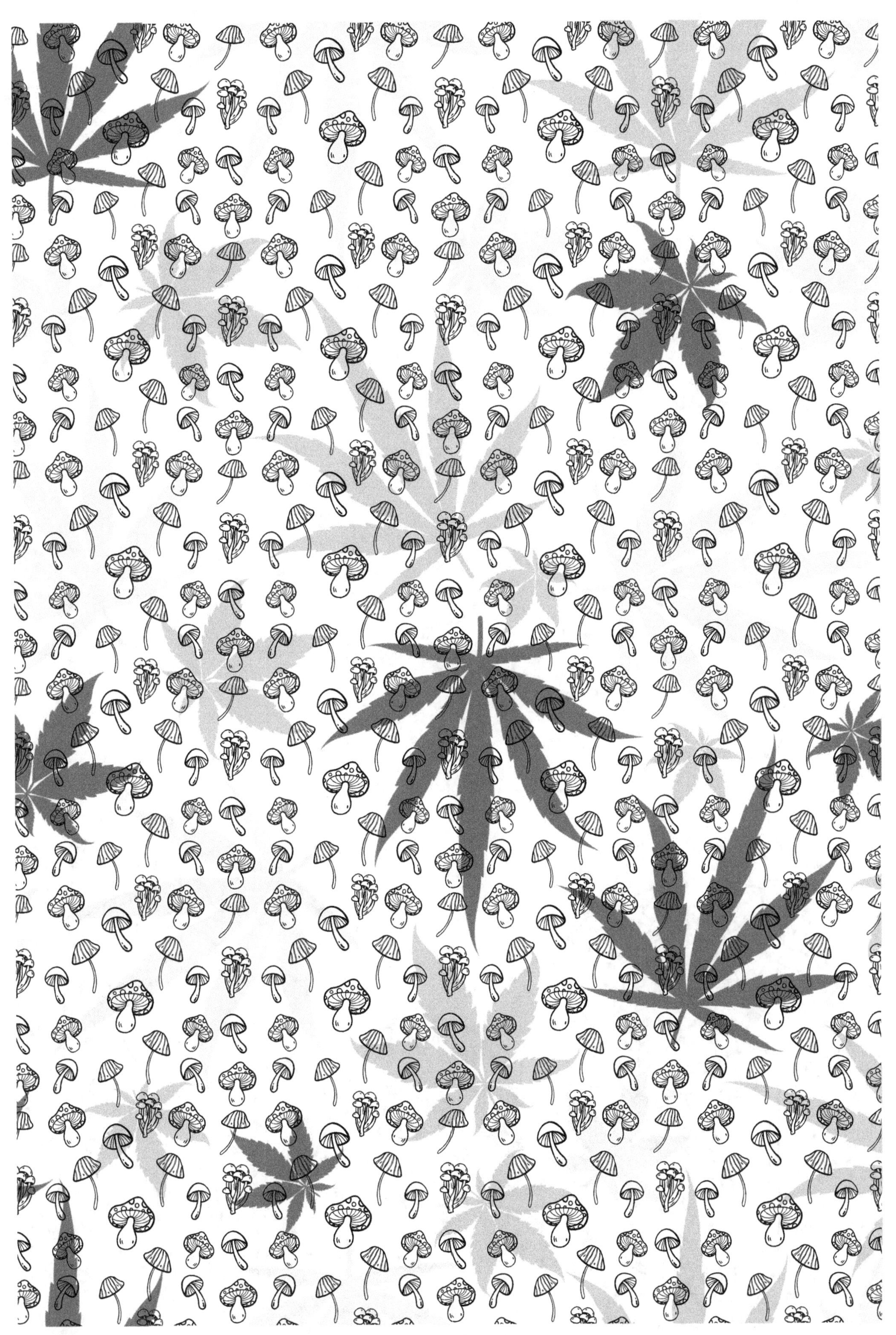

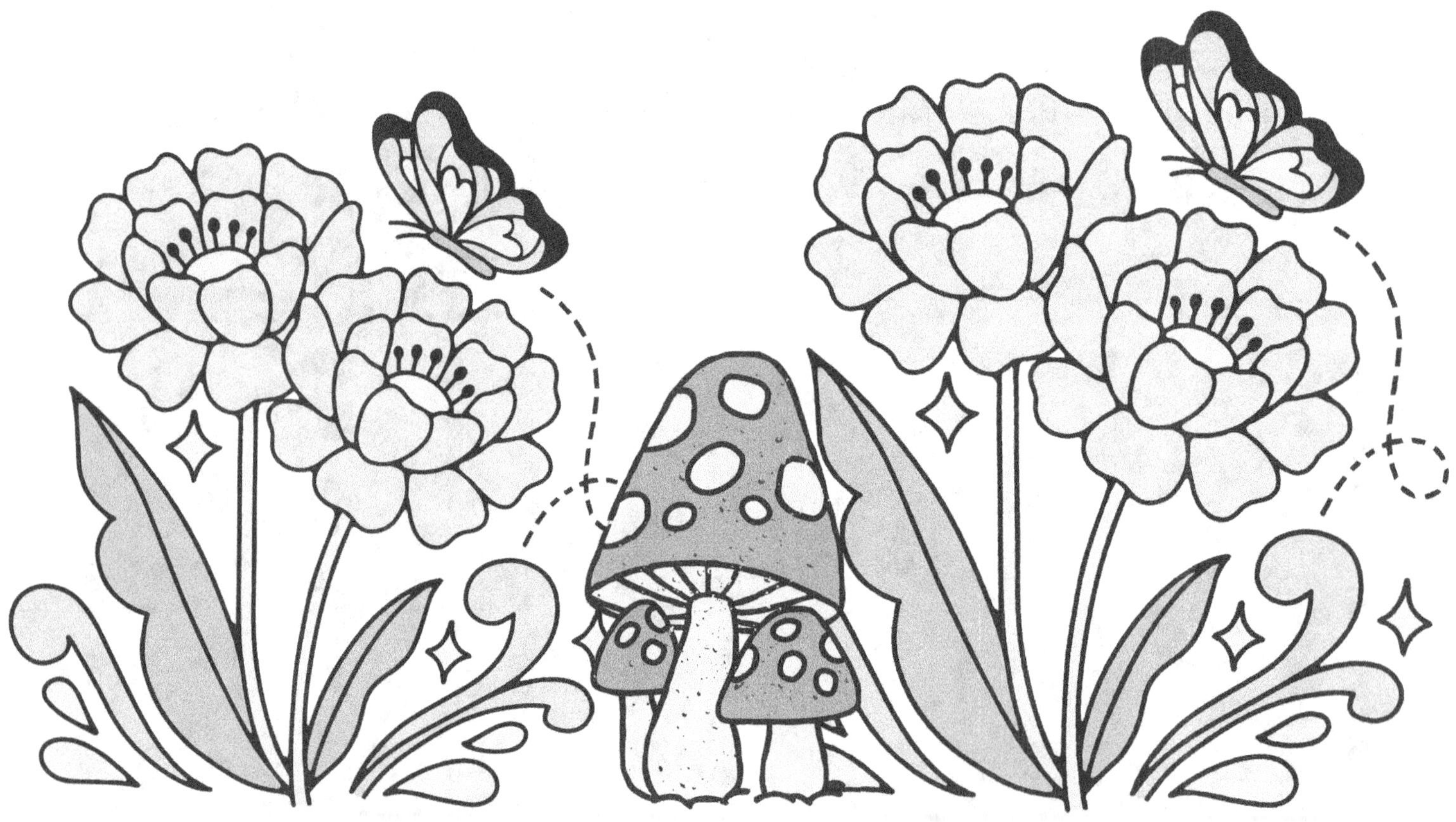
THROUGH

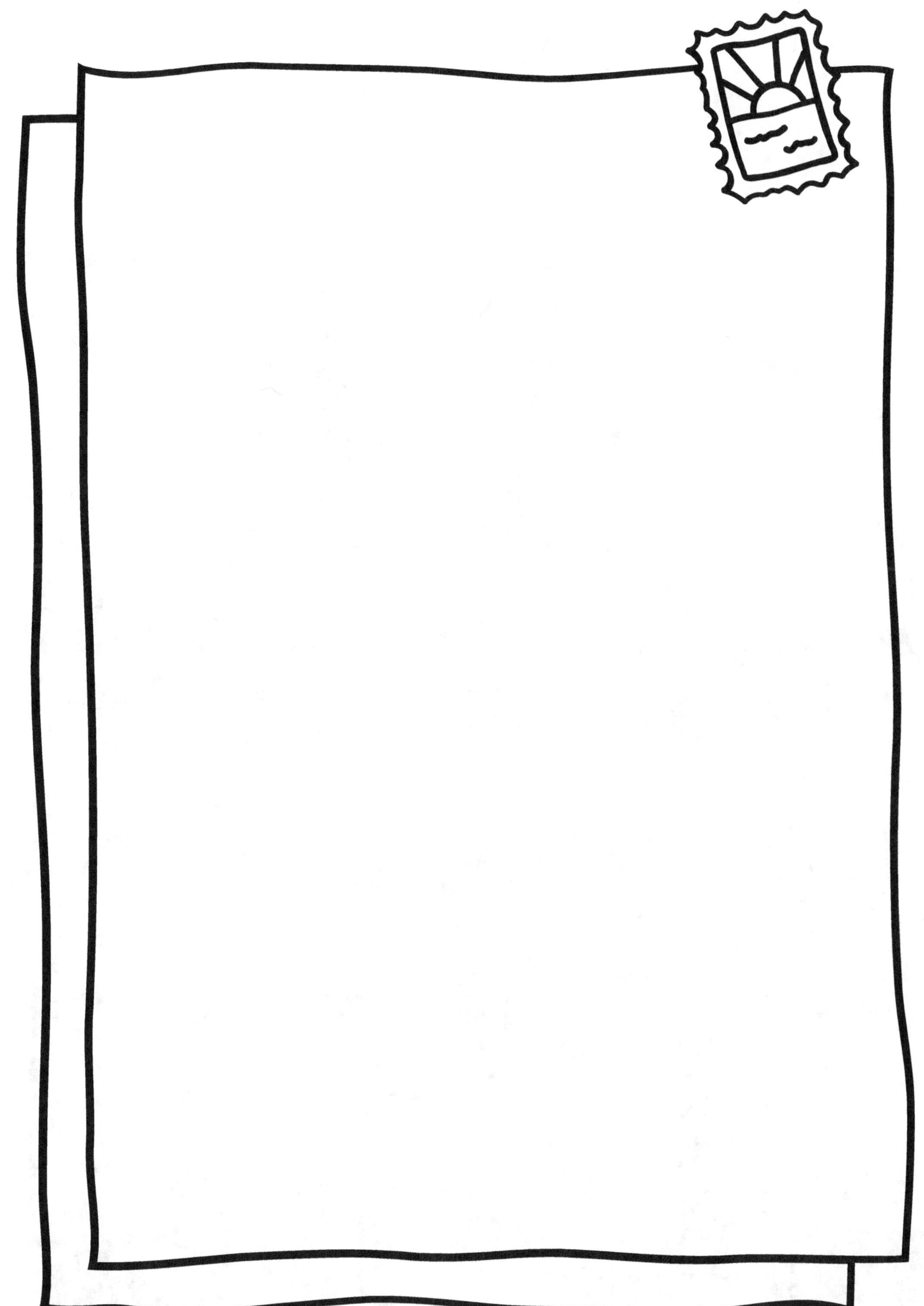

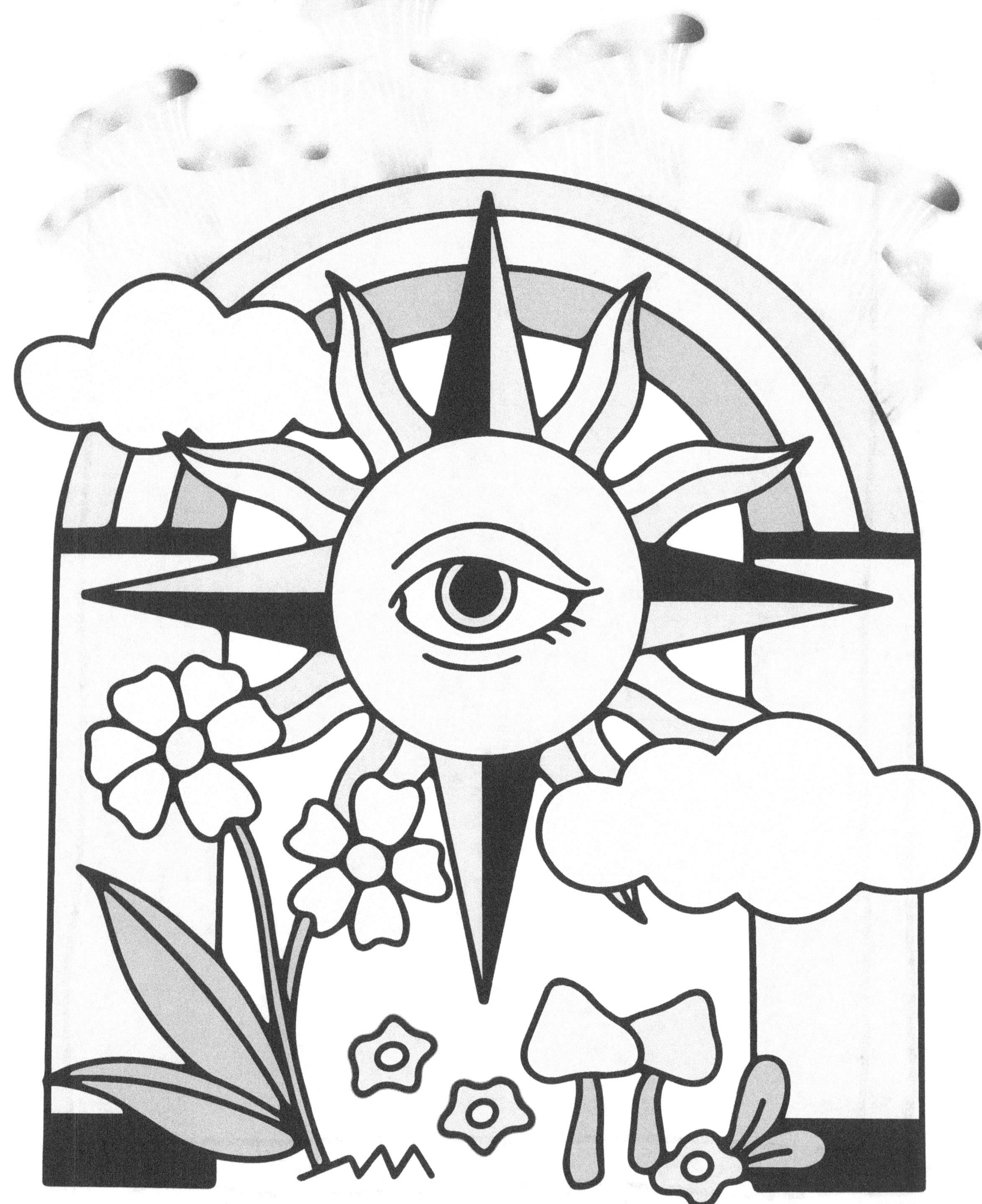

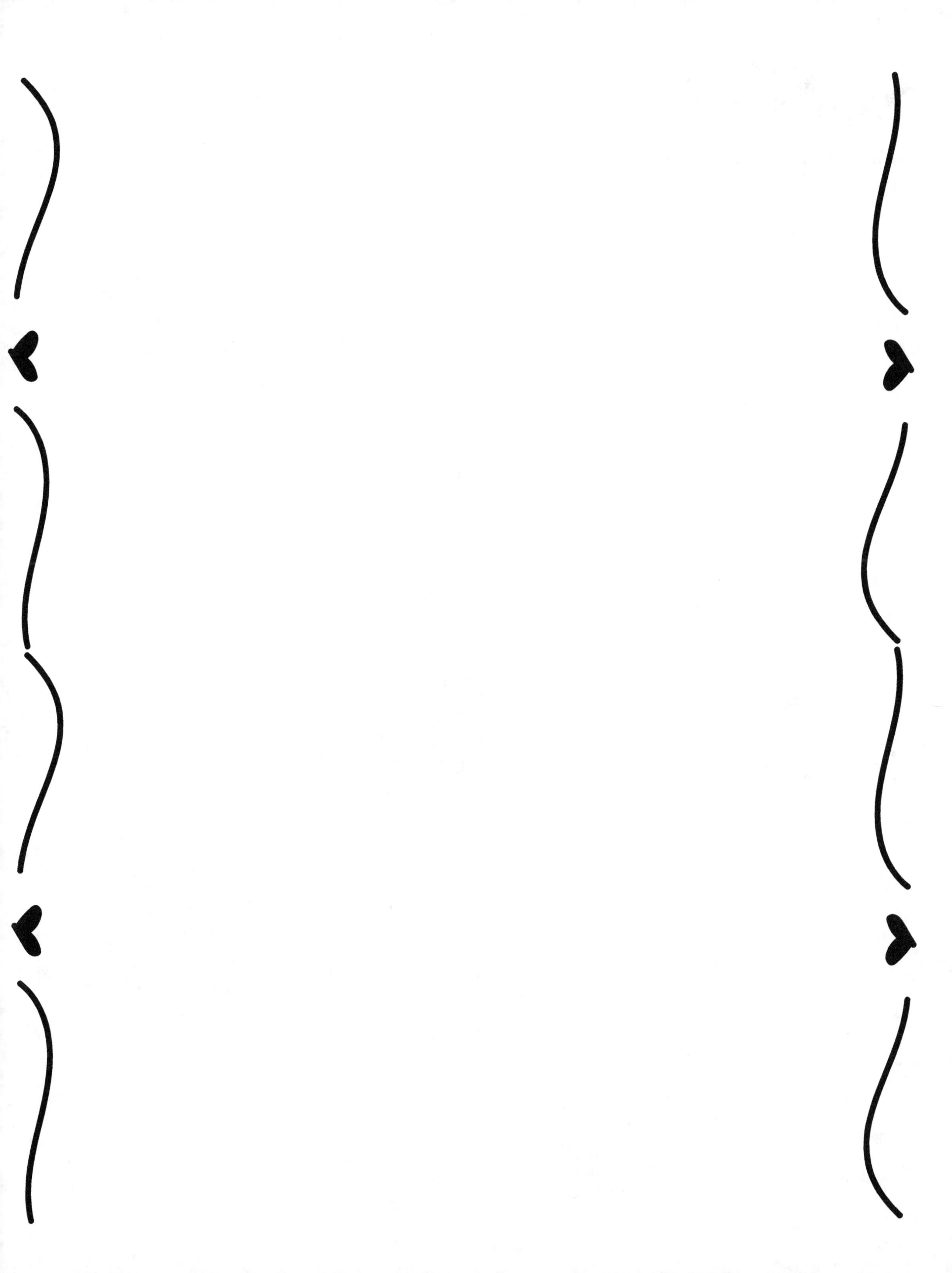

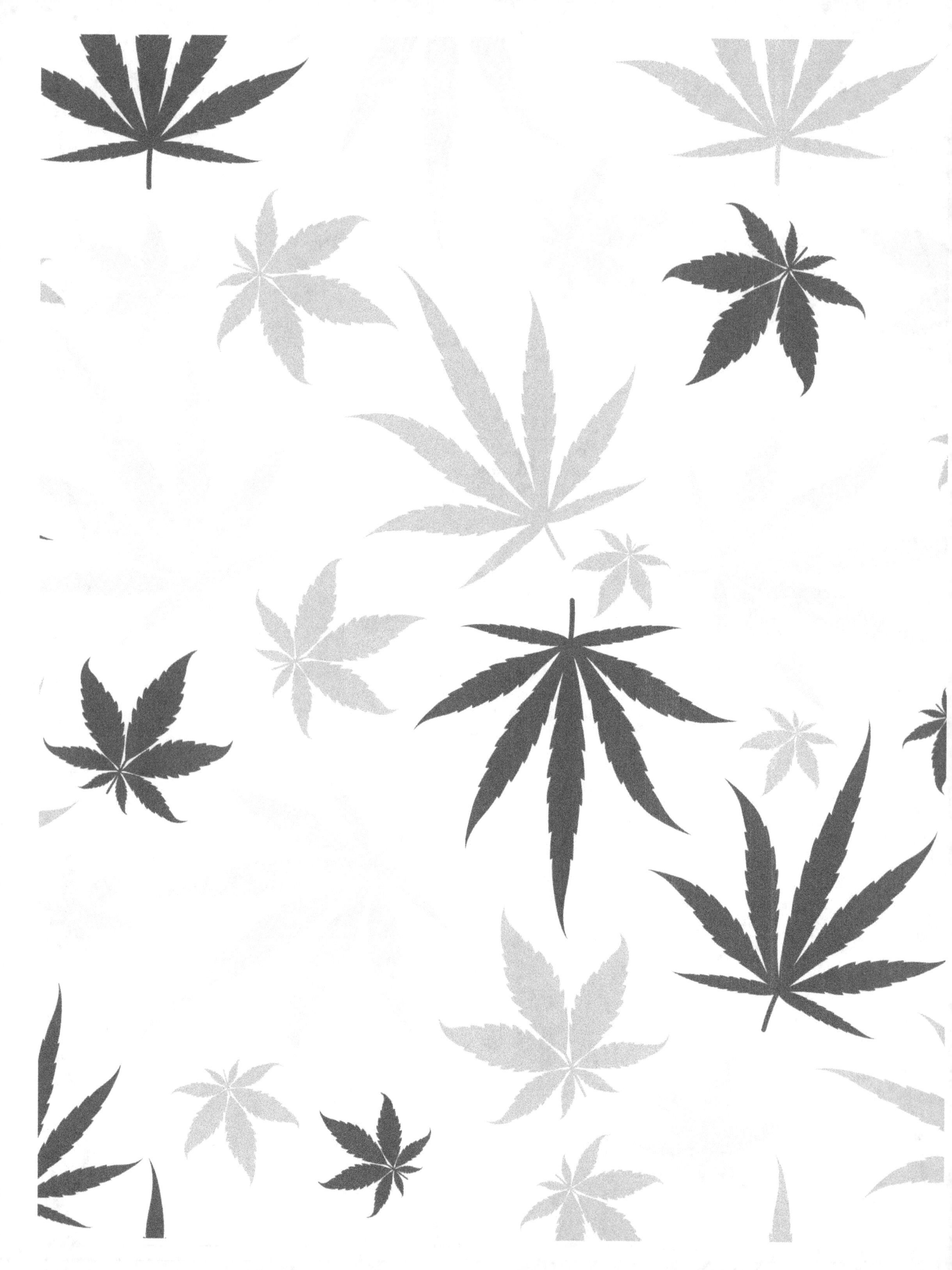

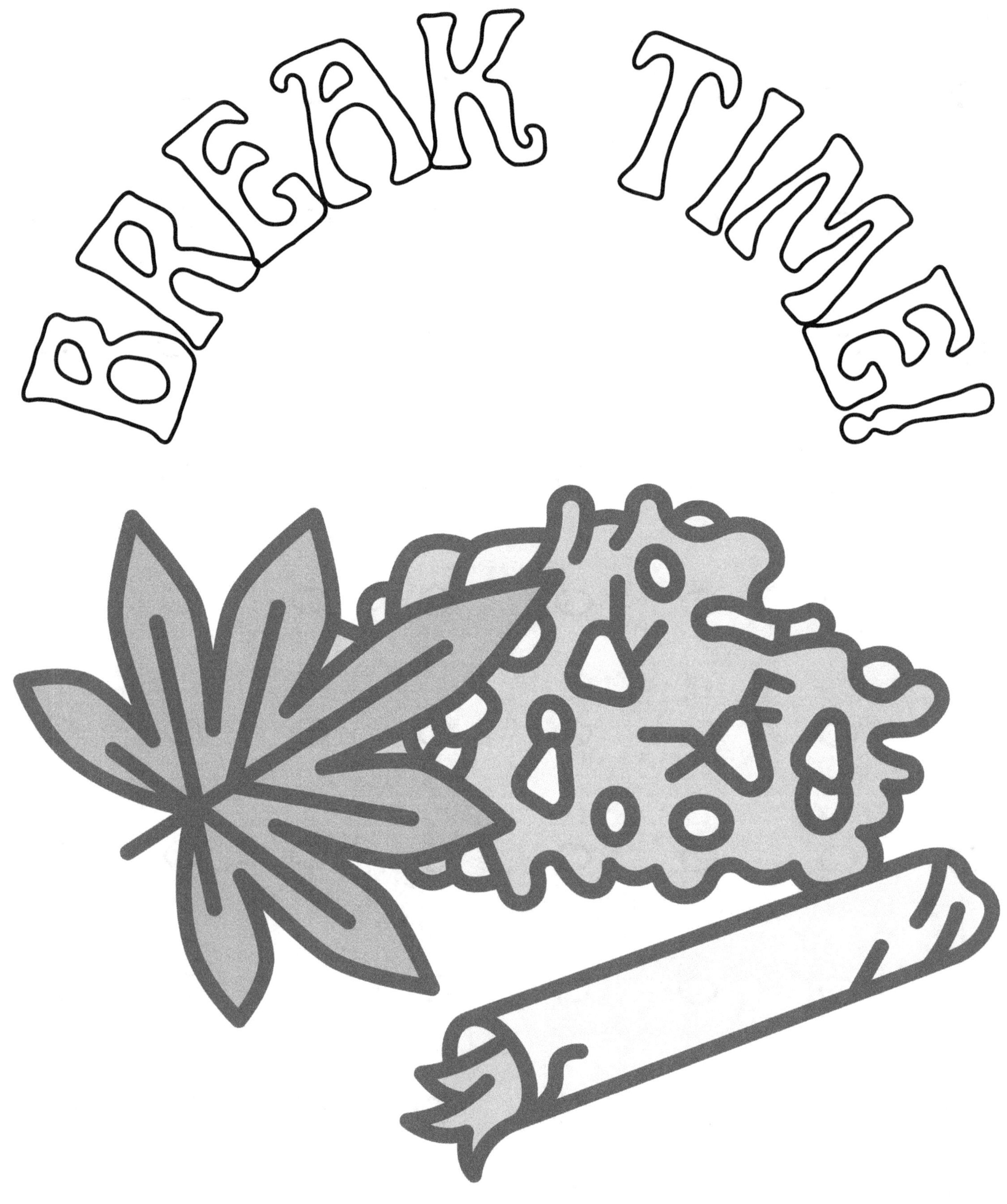

BREAK TIME!

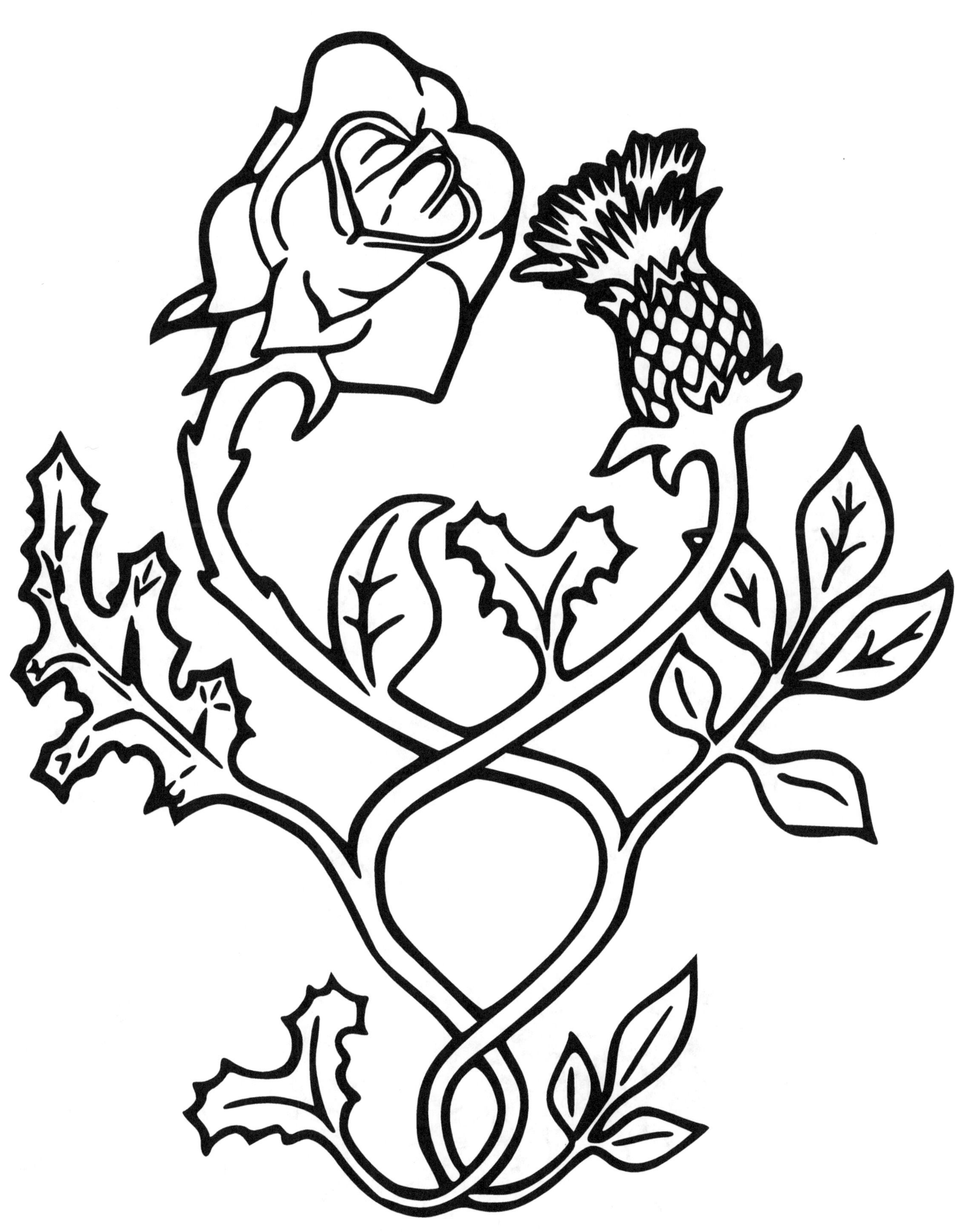

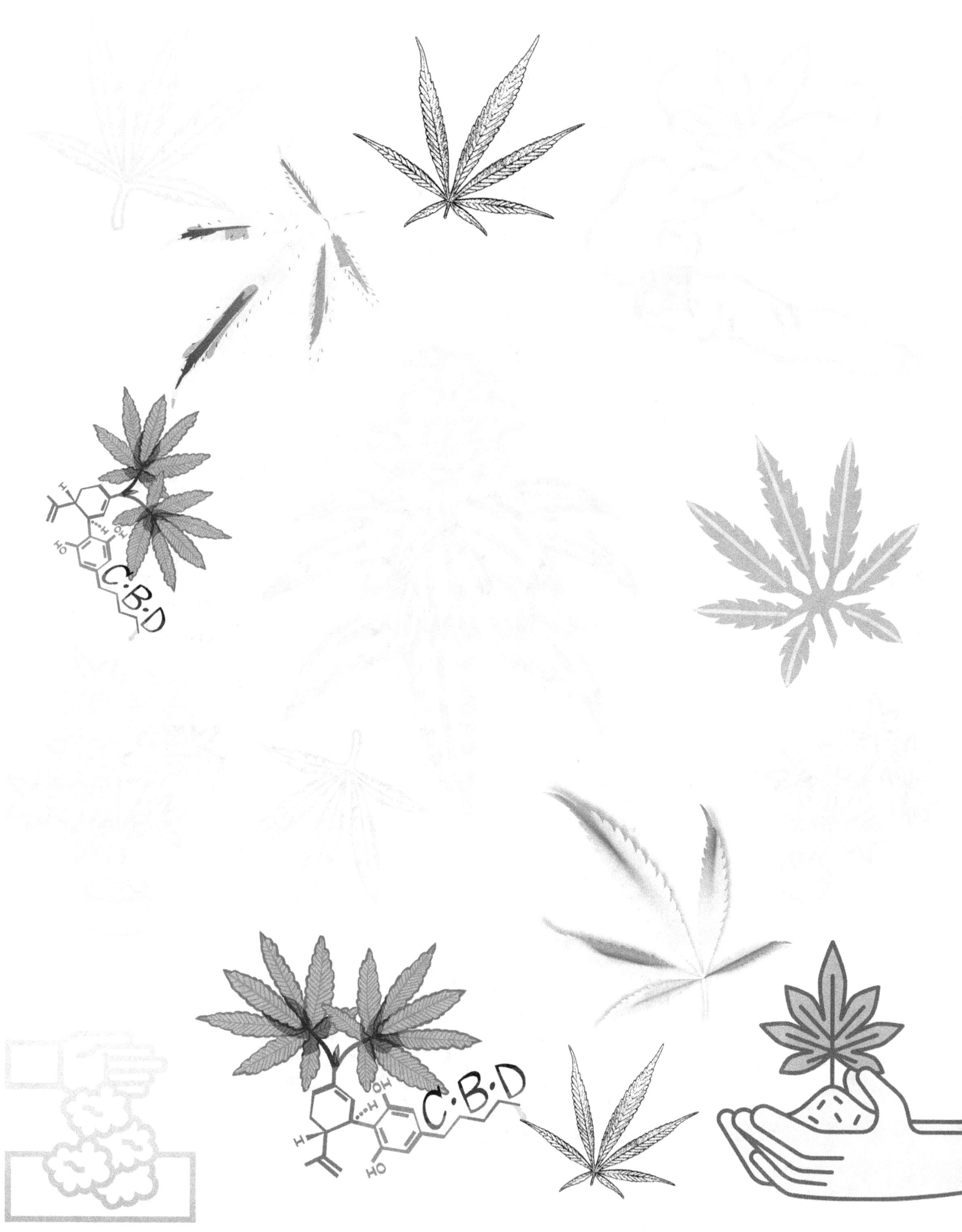

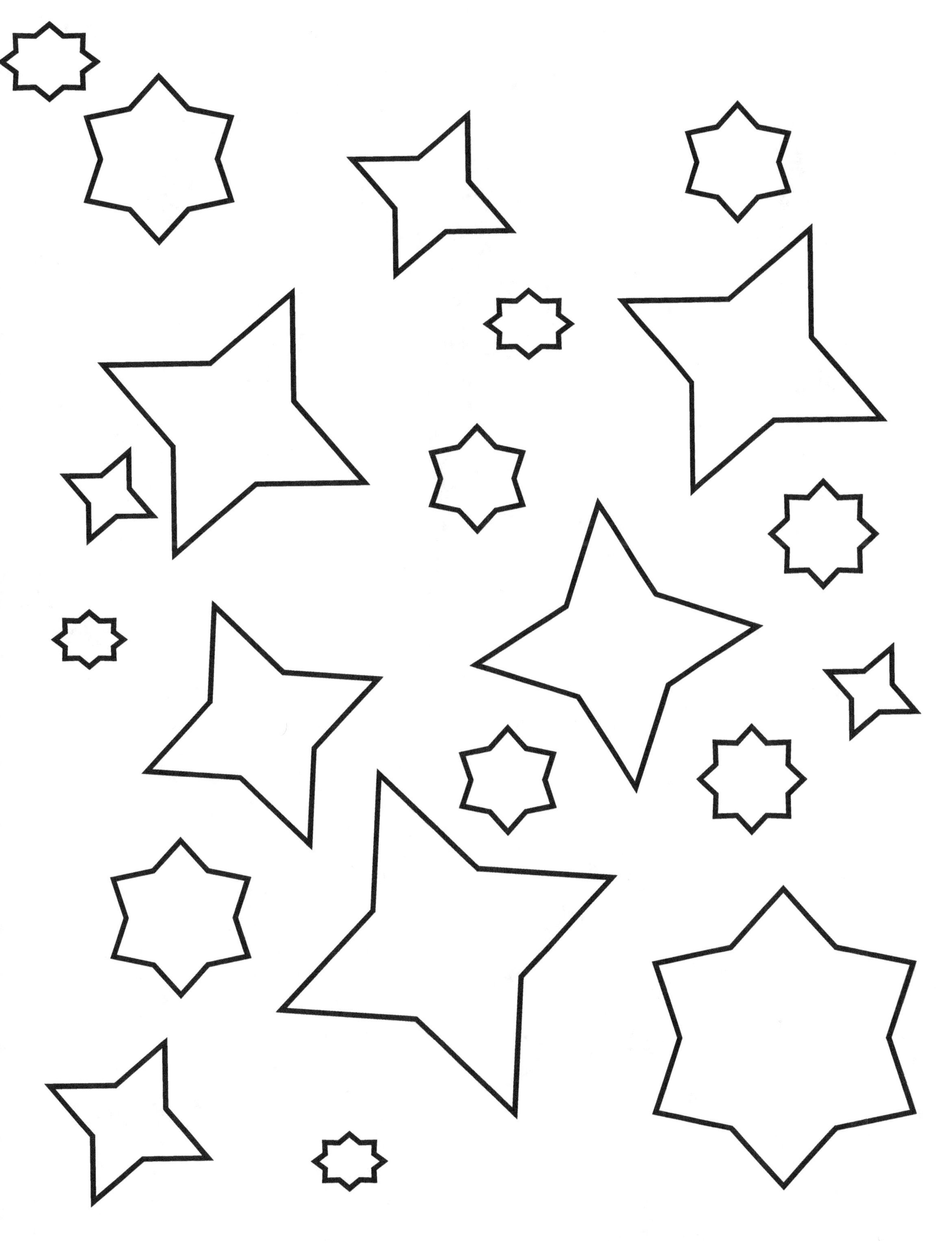

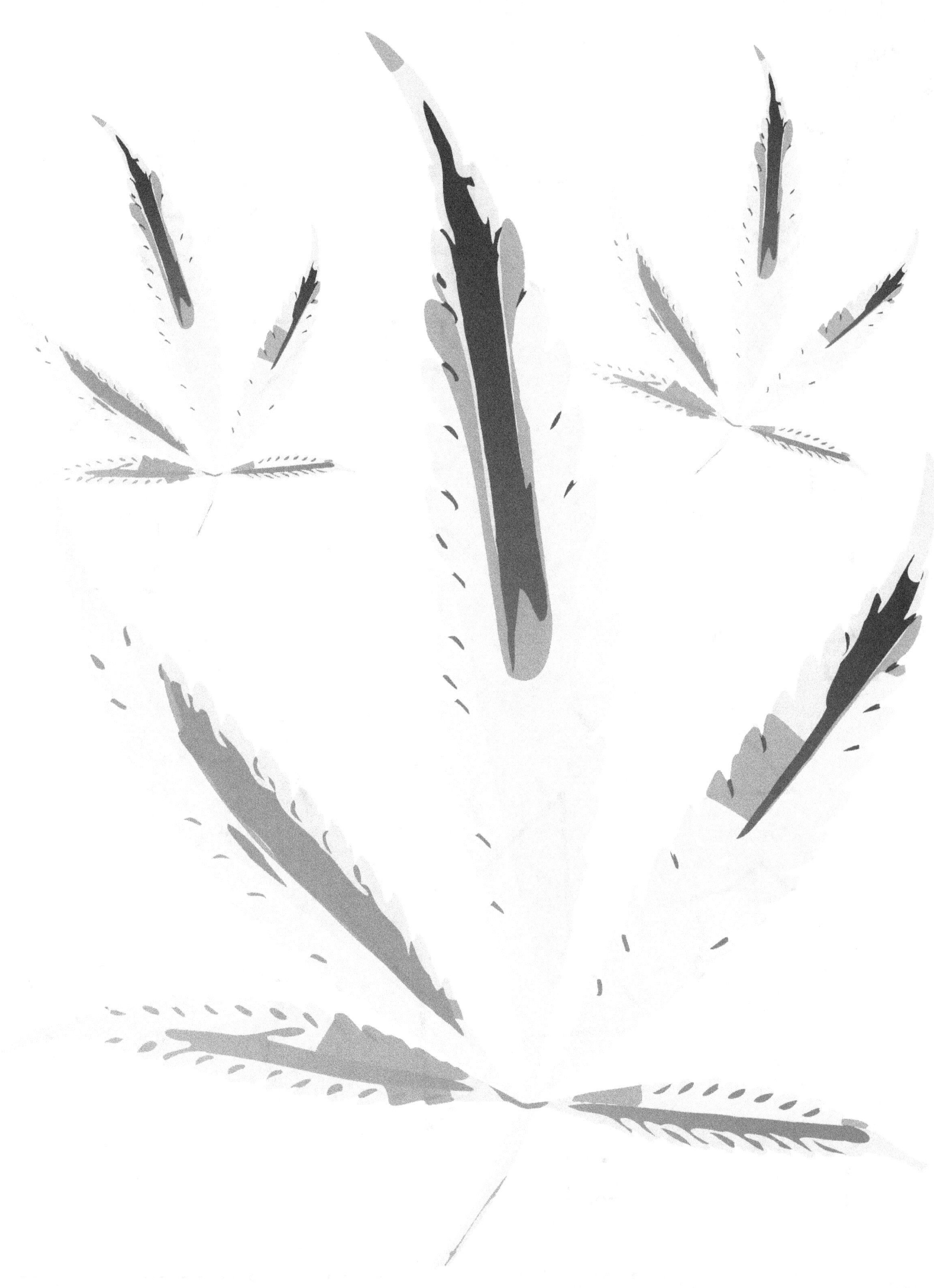

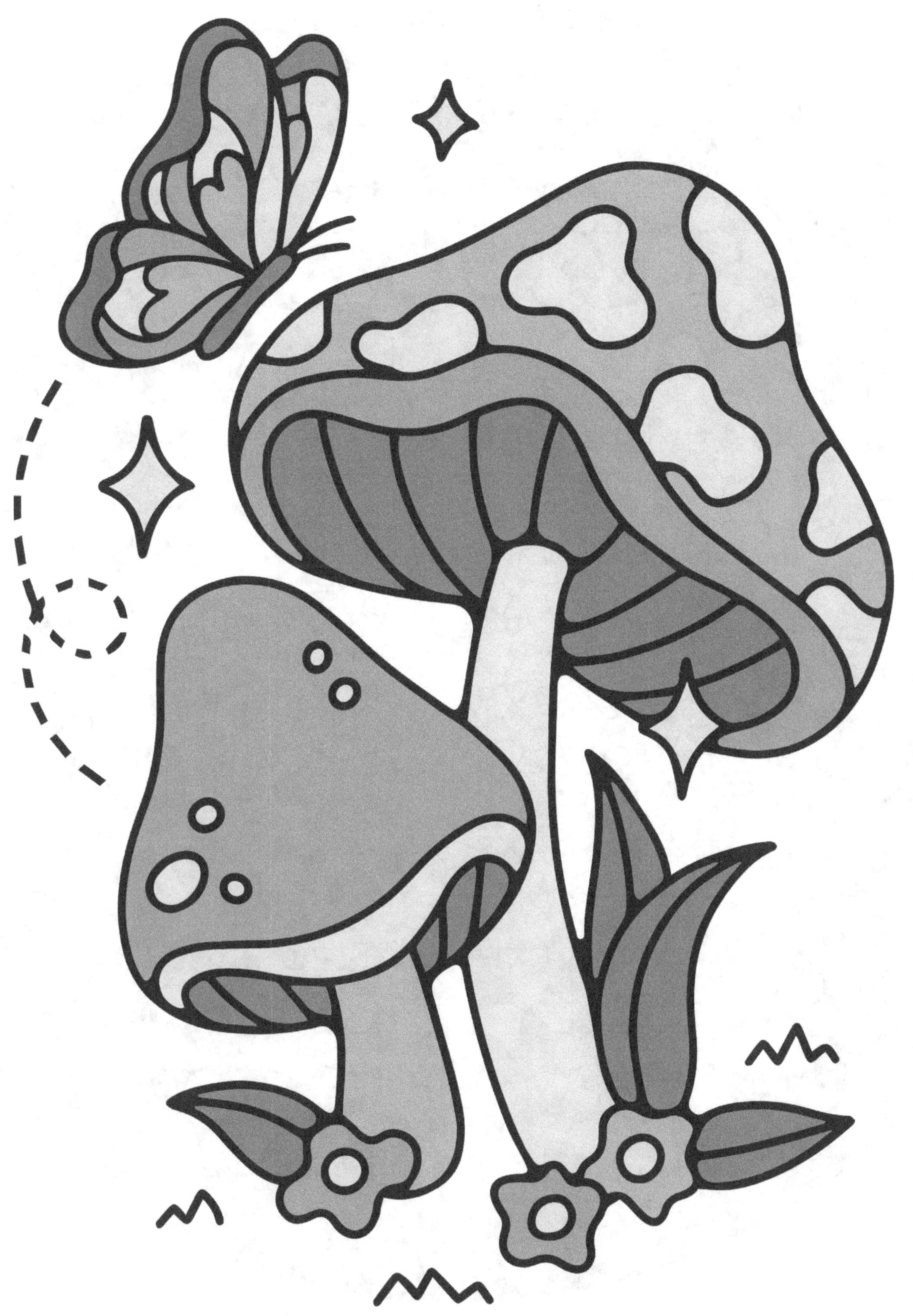

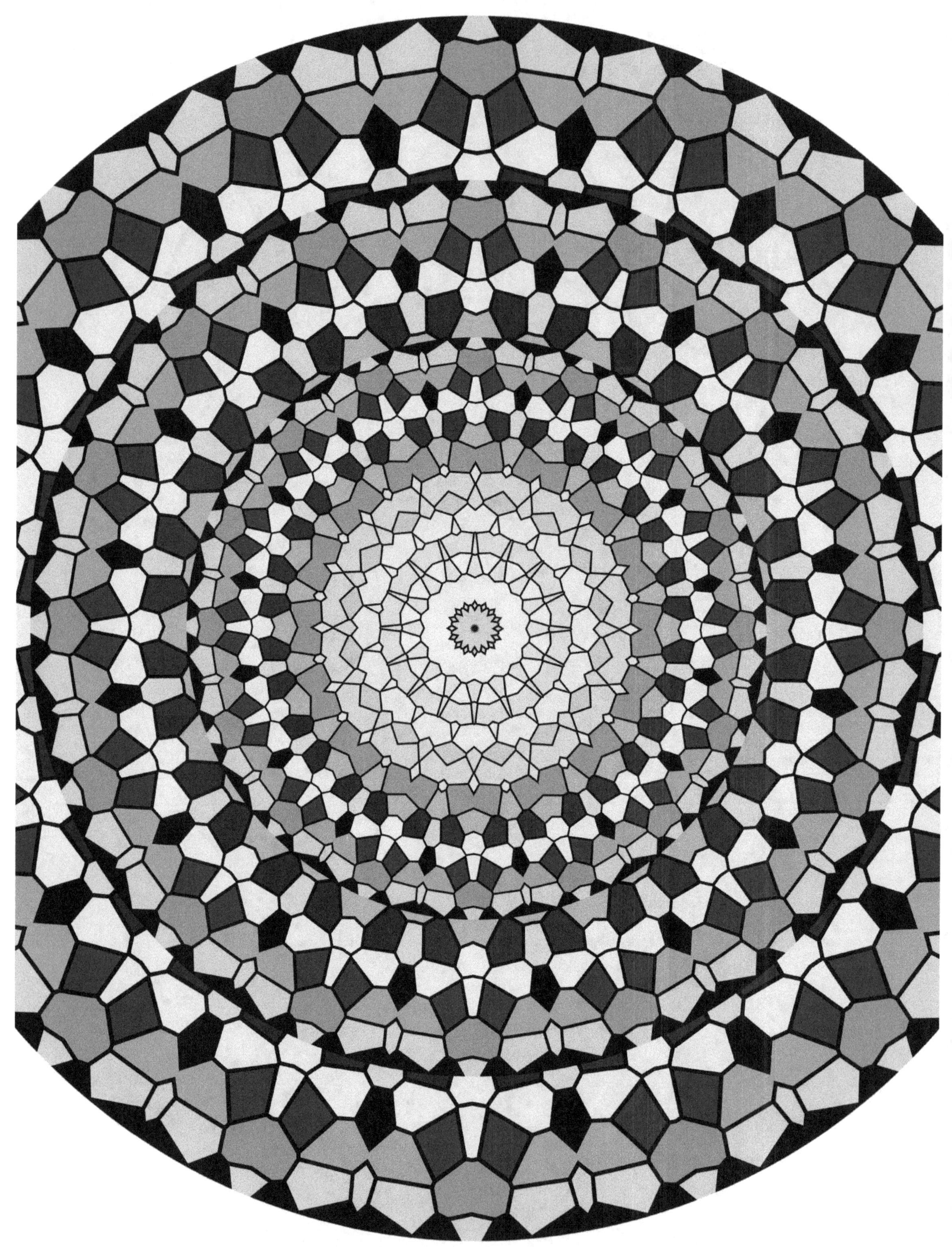

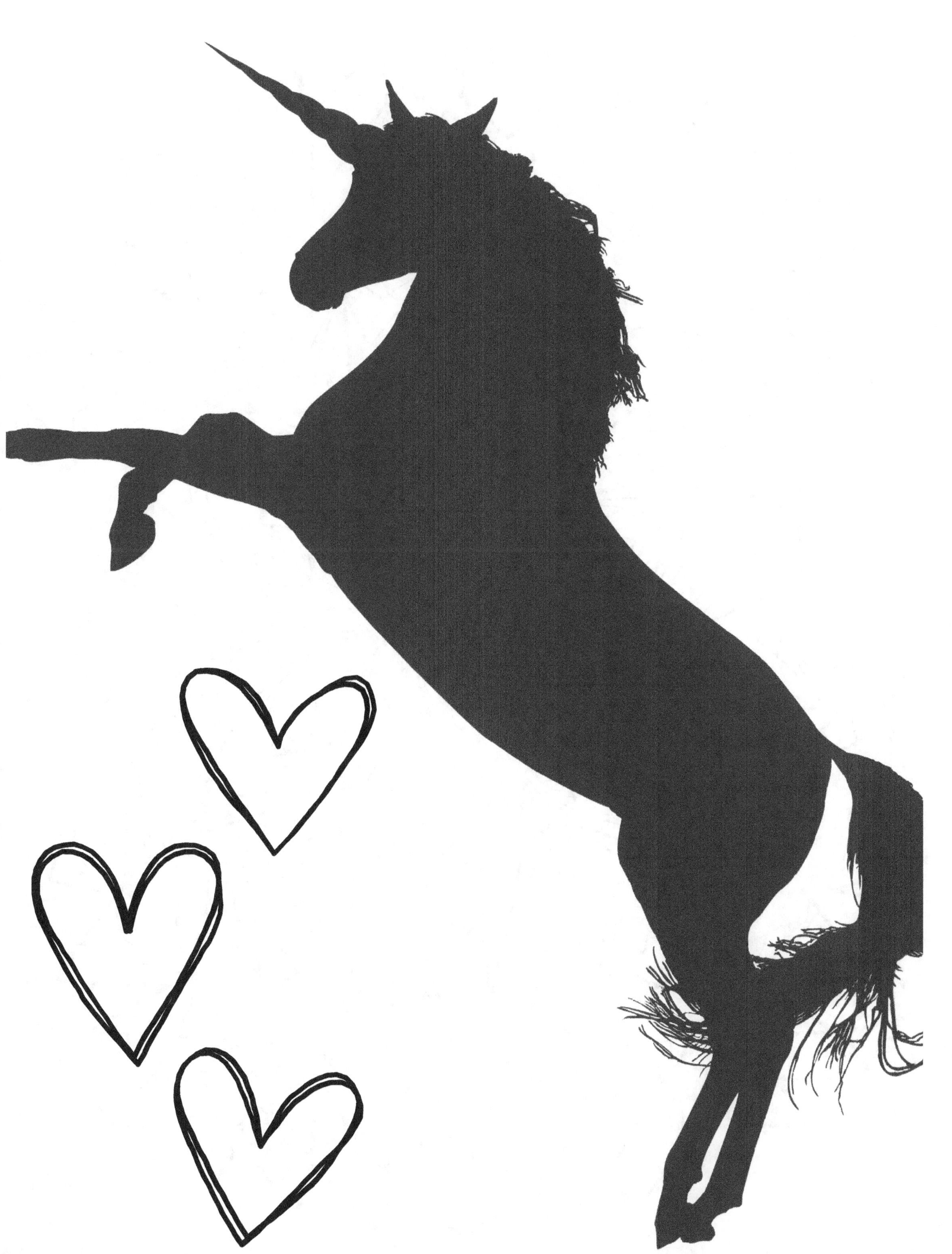

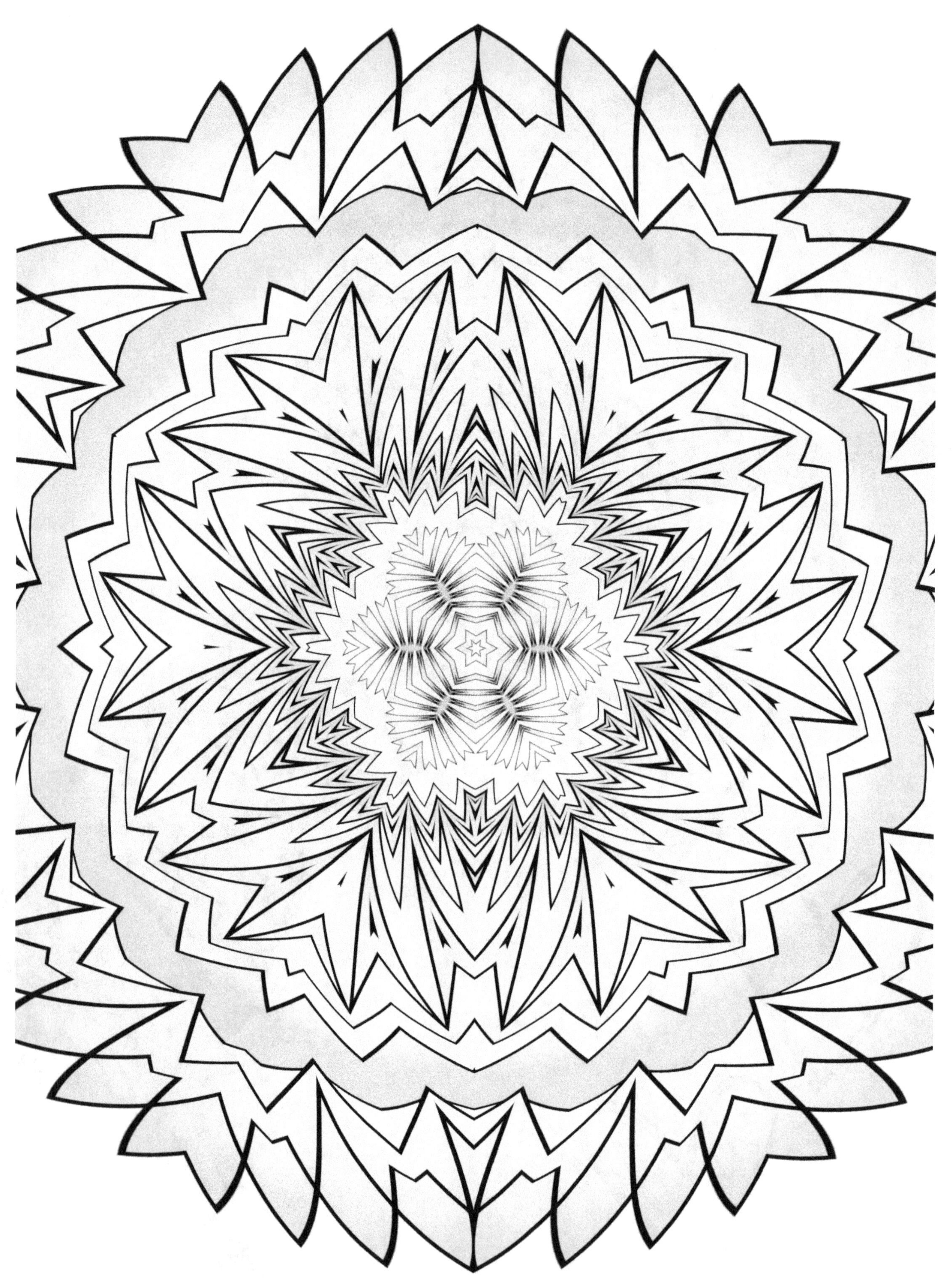

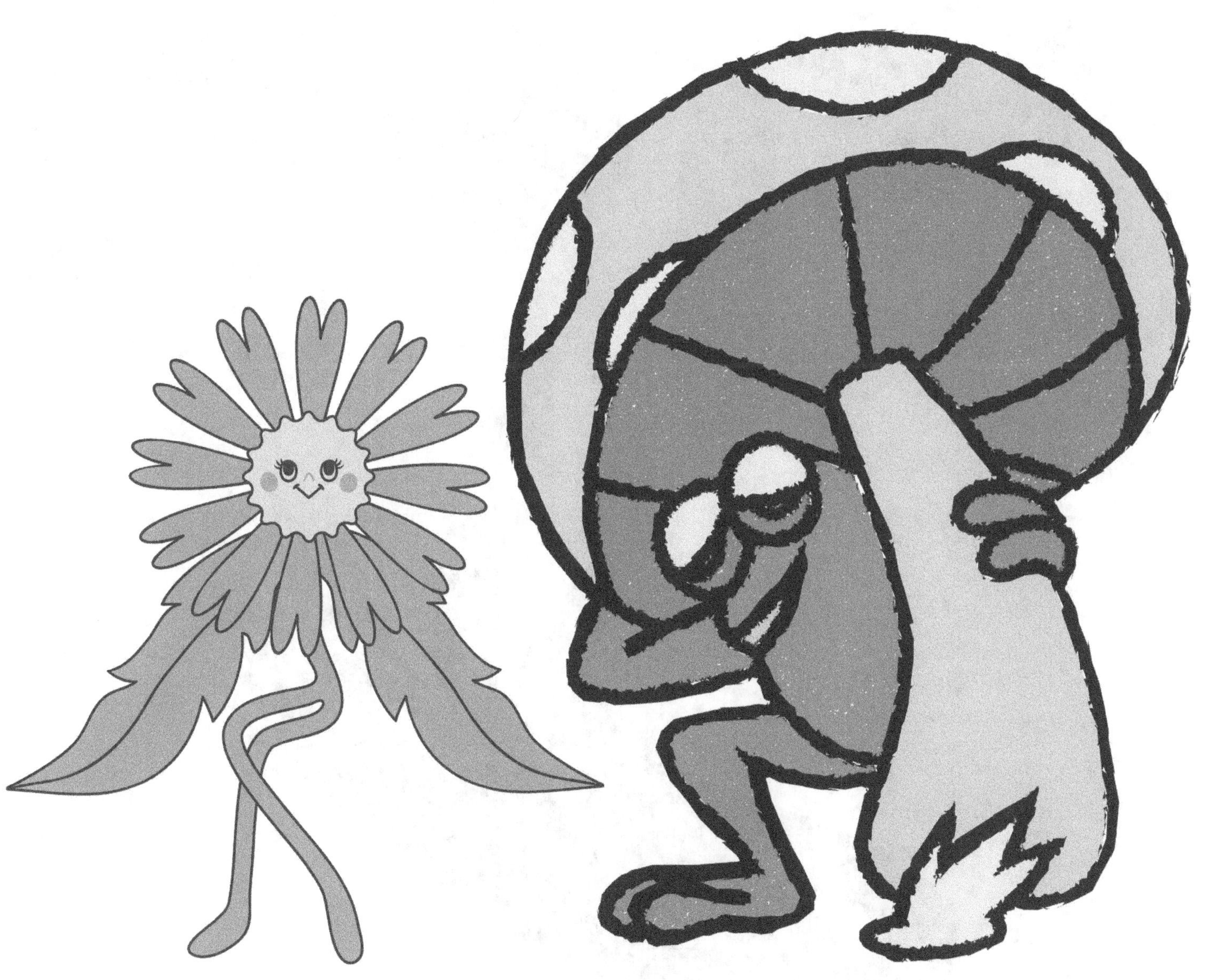

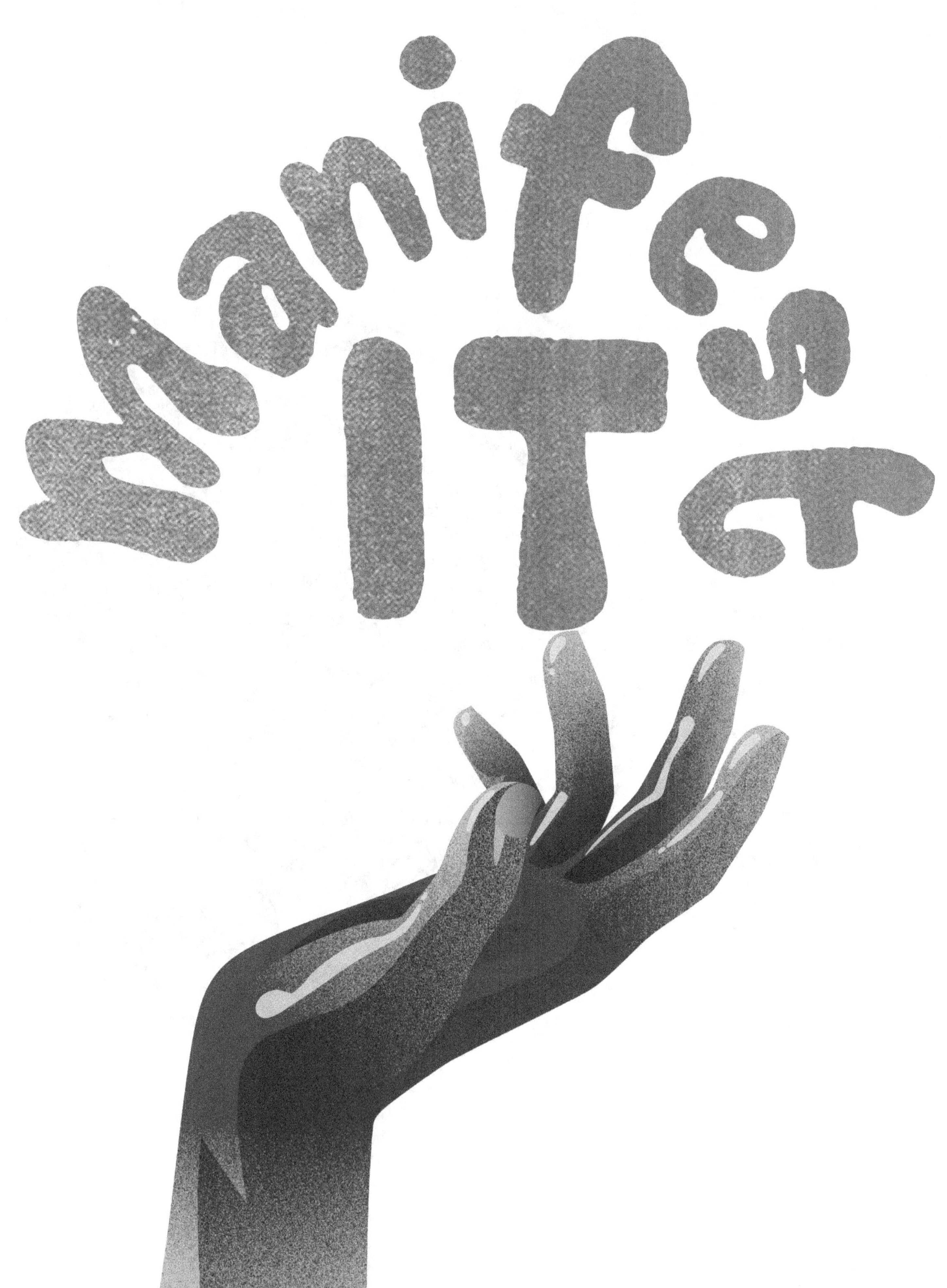

Manifest
IT

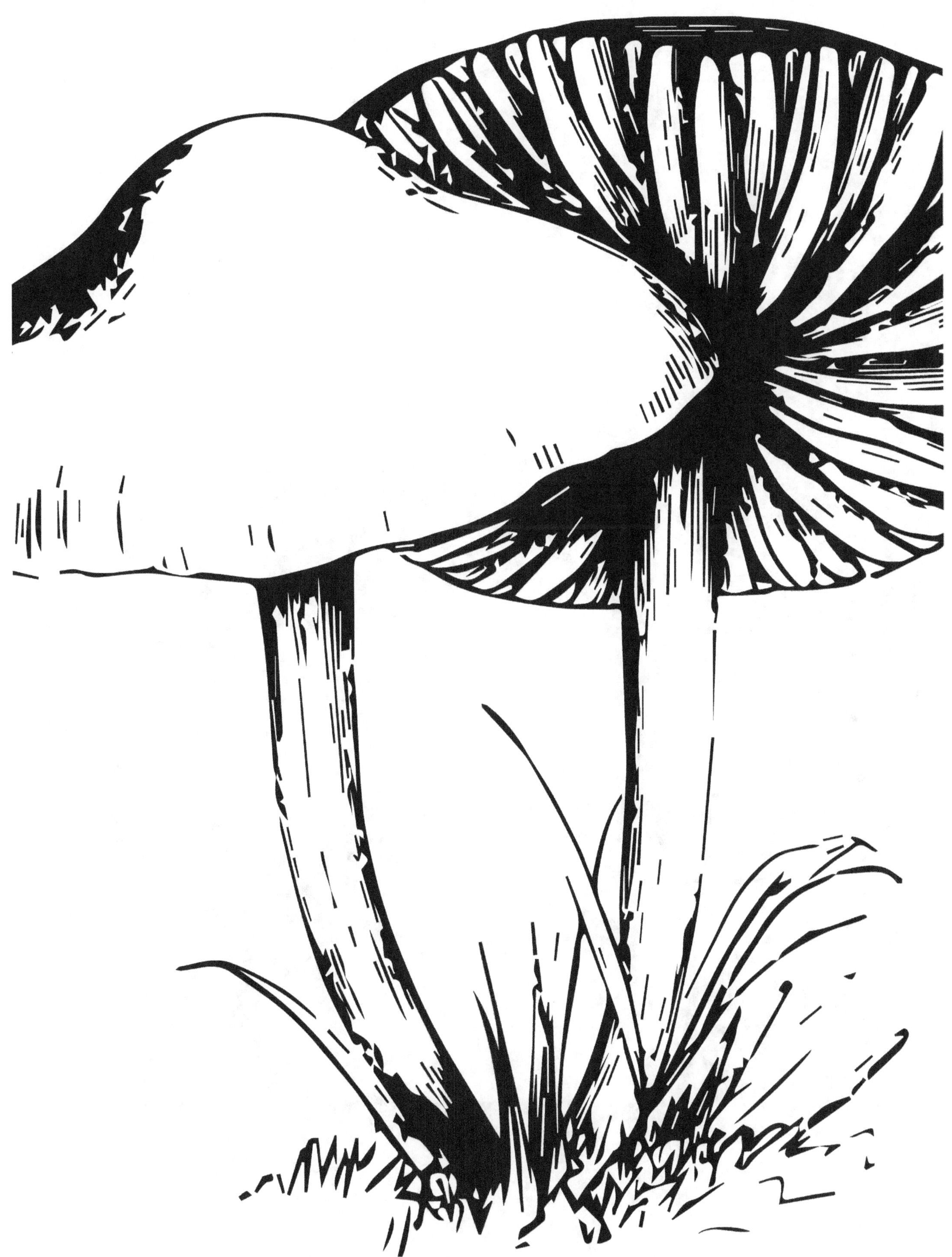

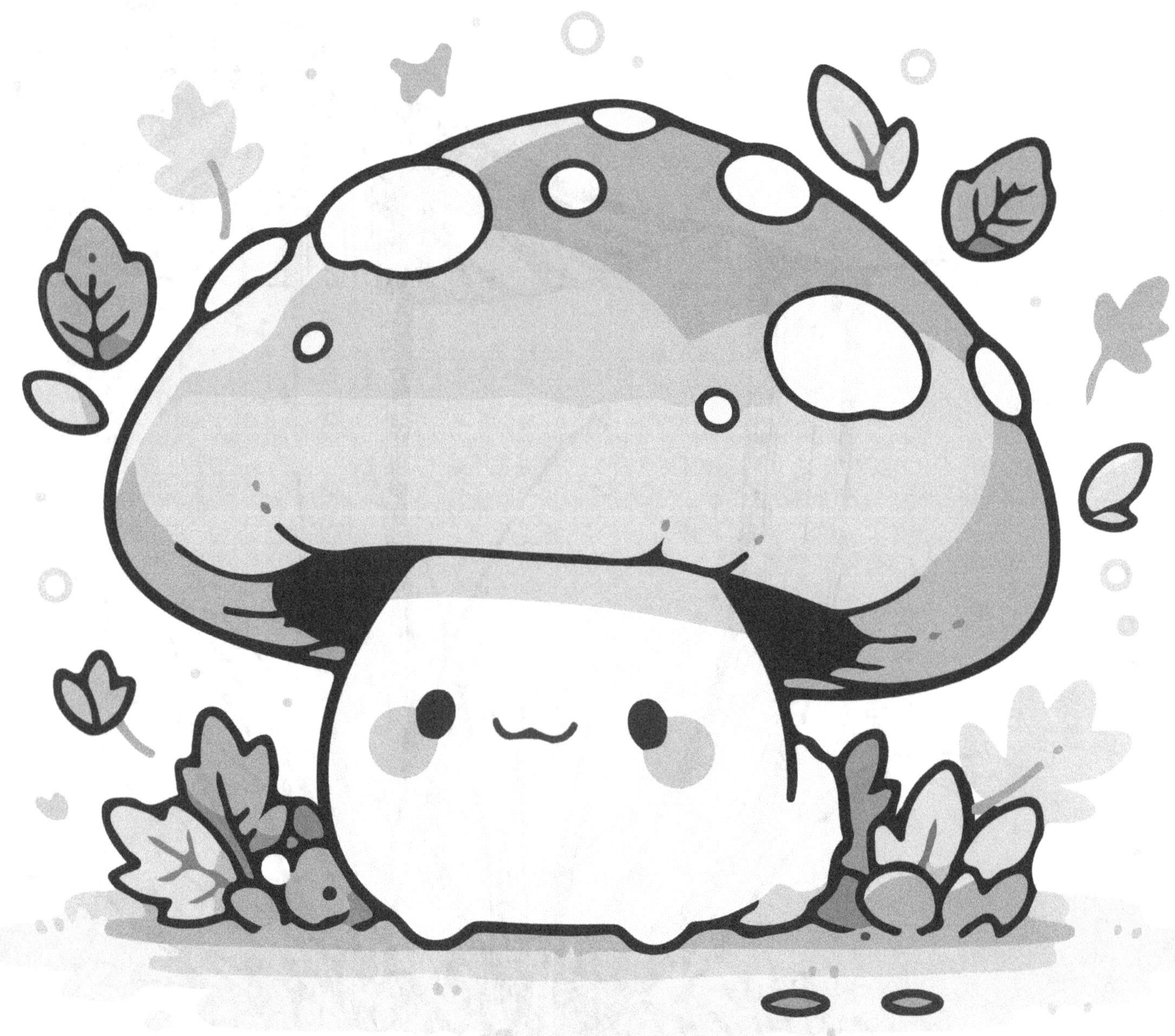

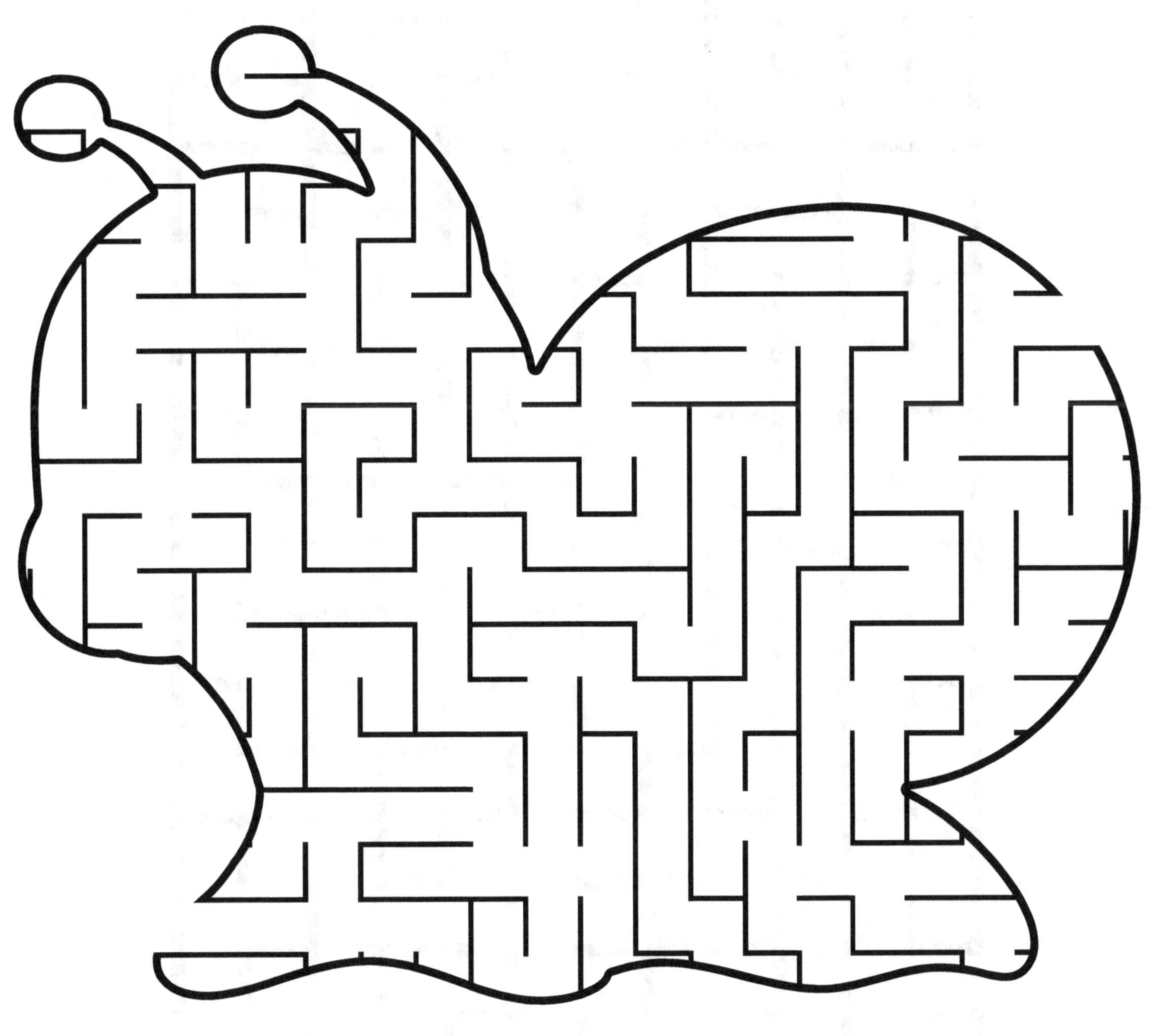

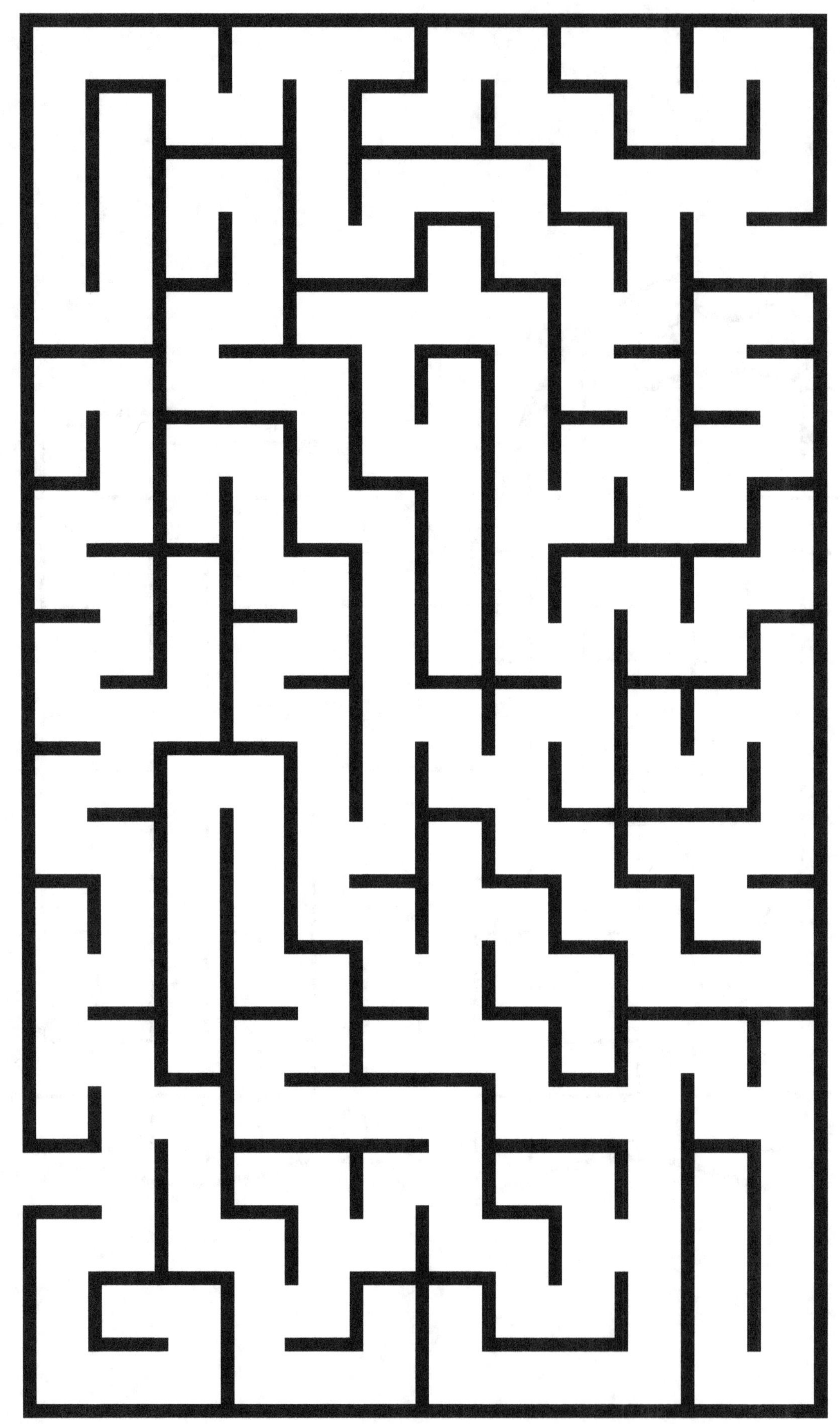

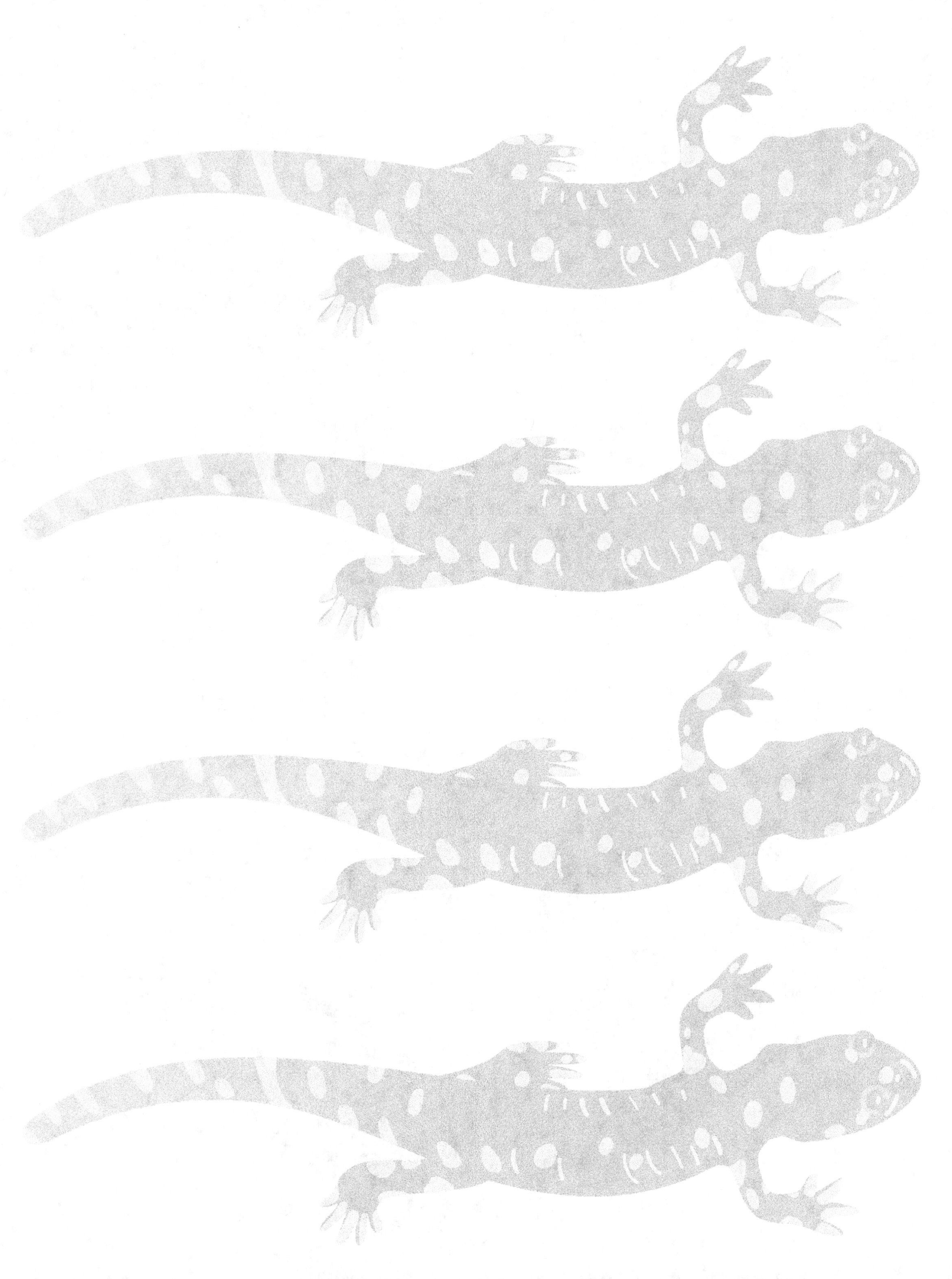

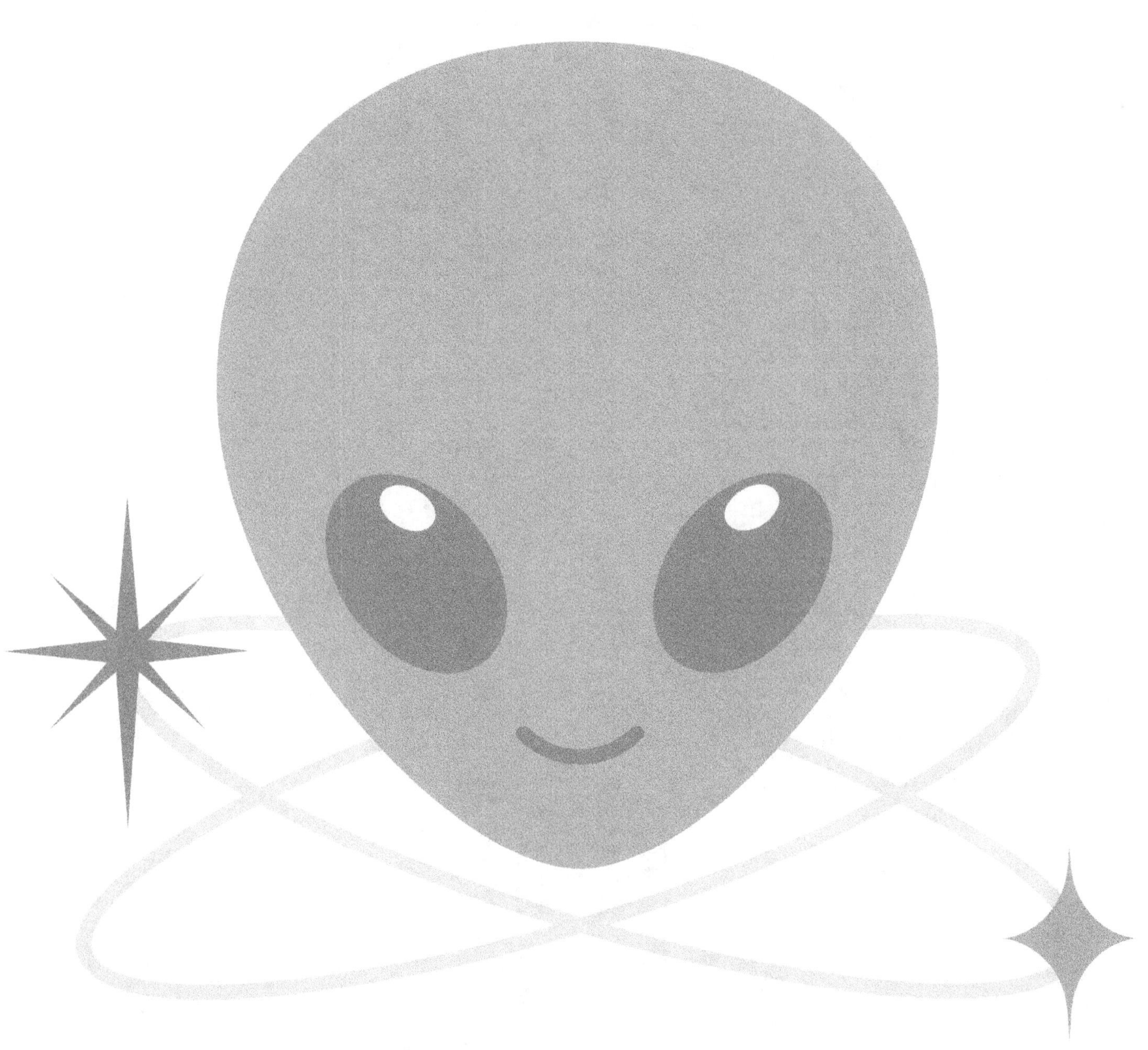

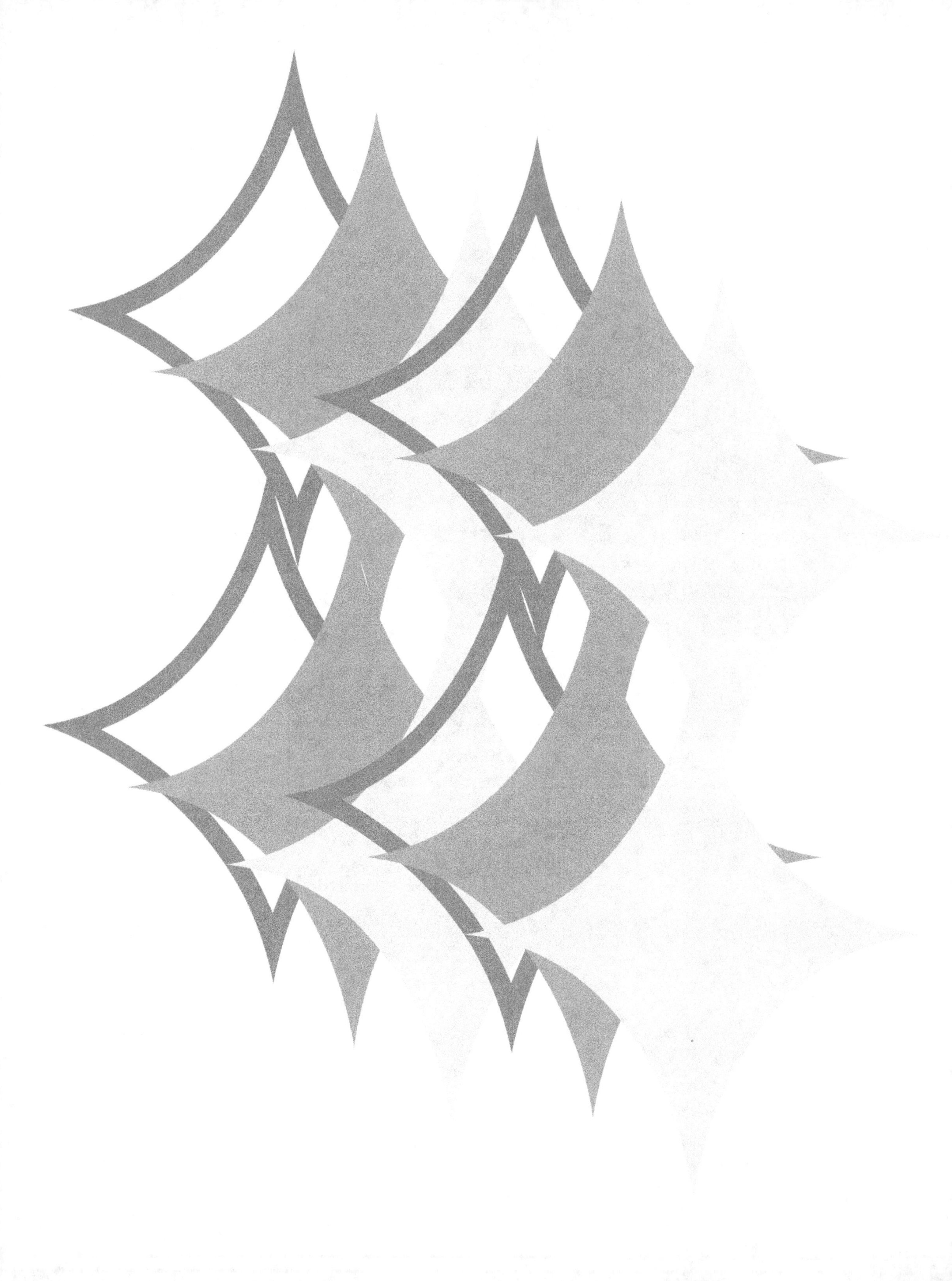

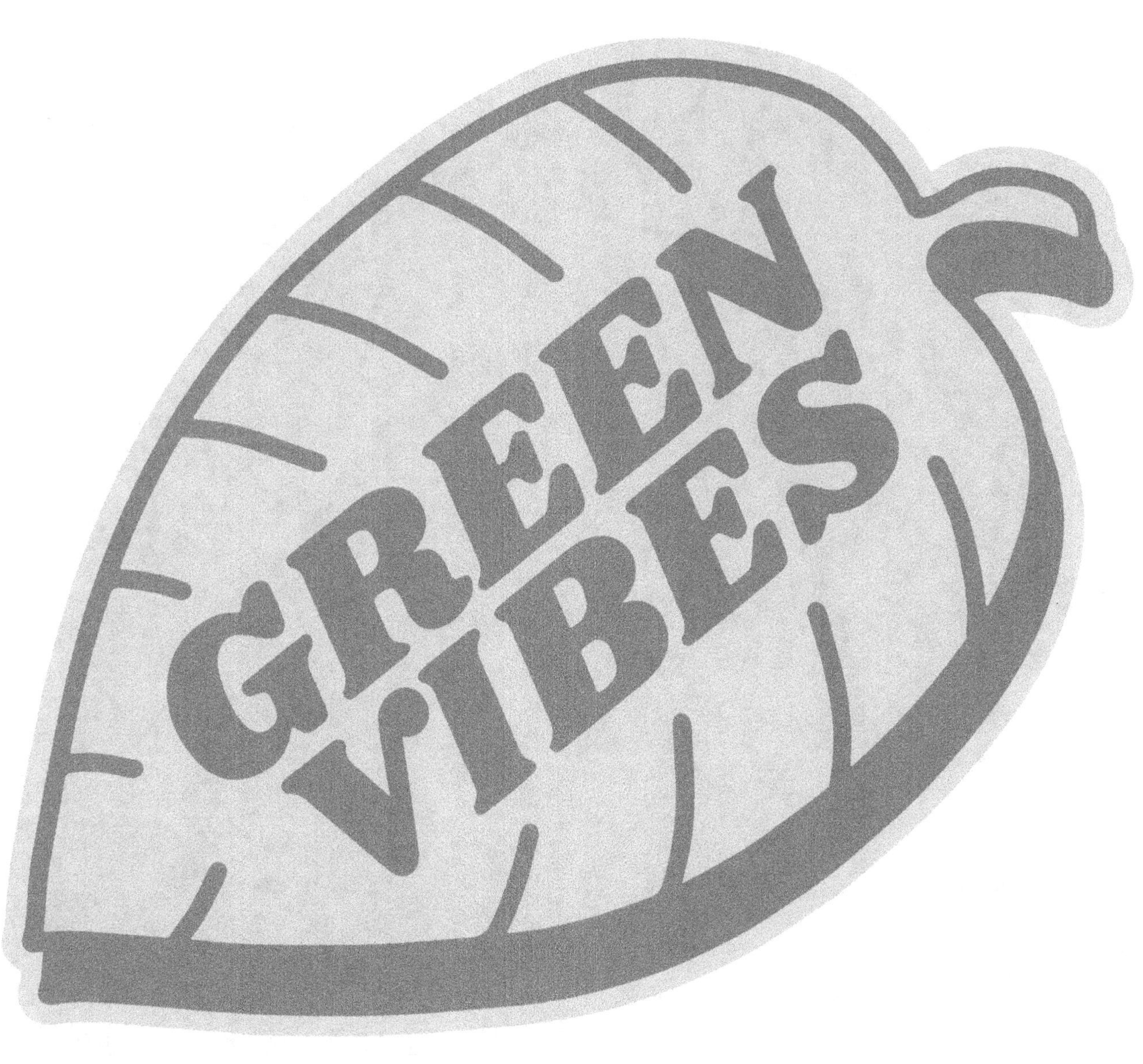

GREEN
VIBES

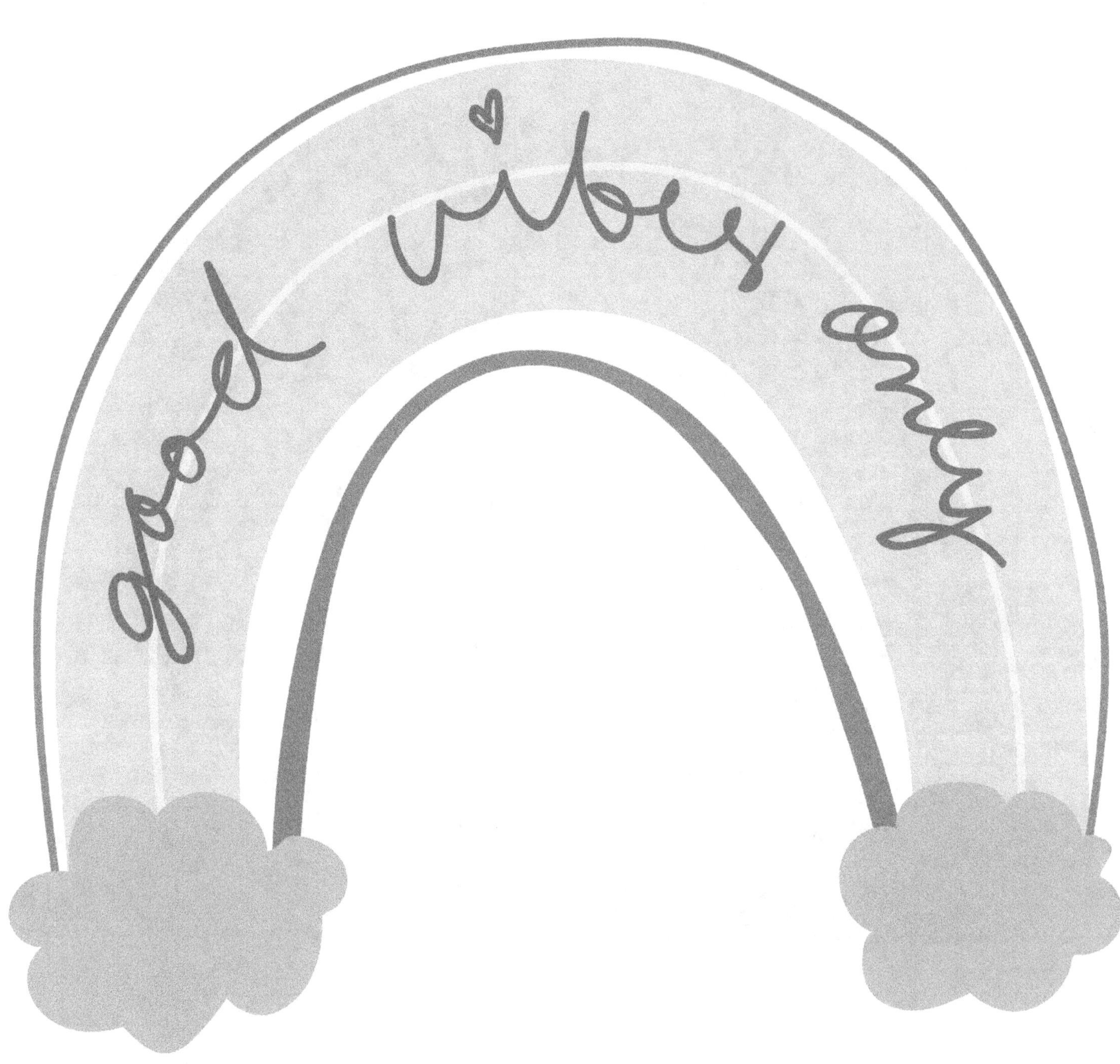

good vibes only

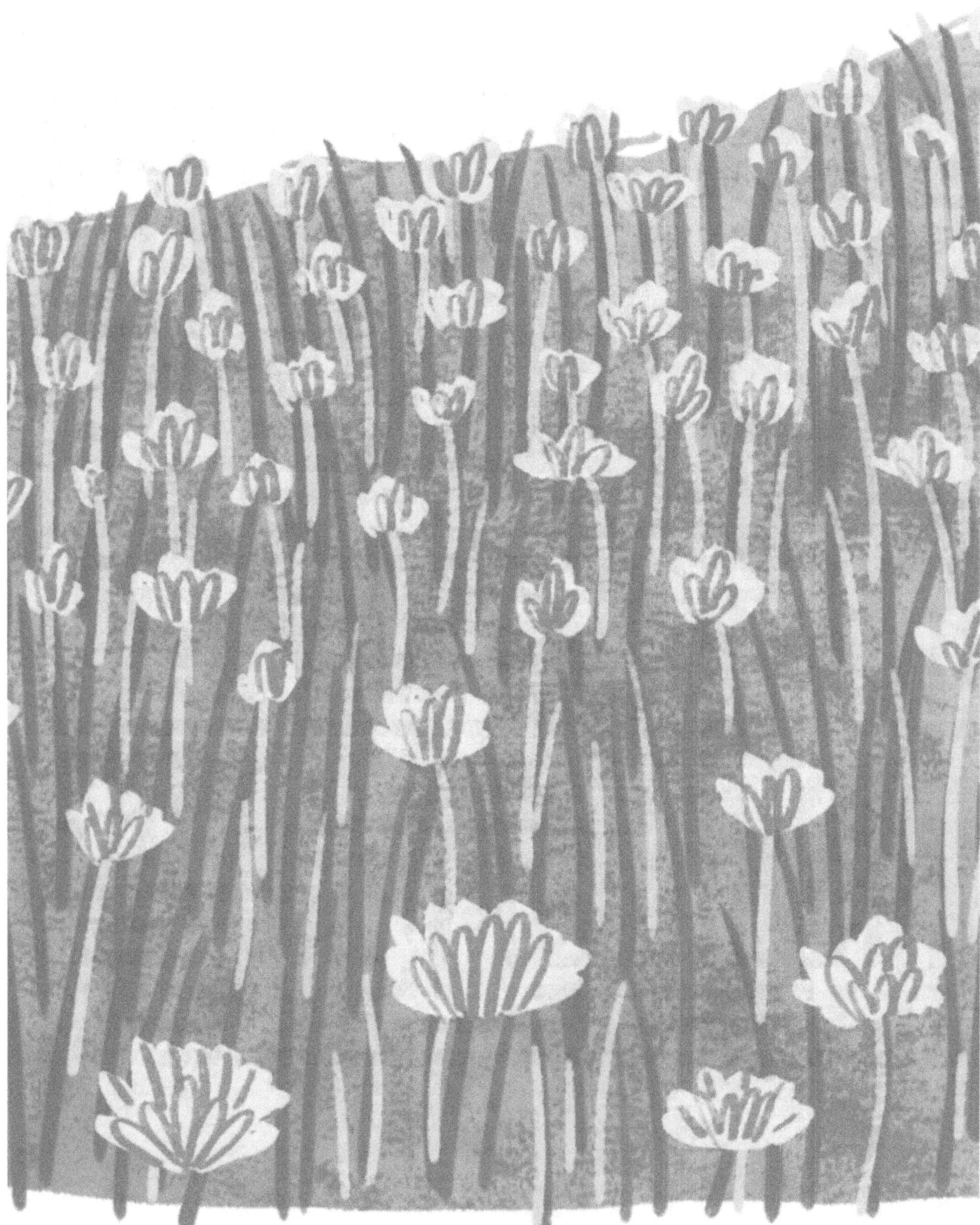

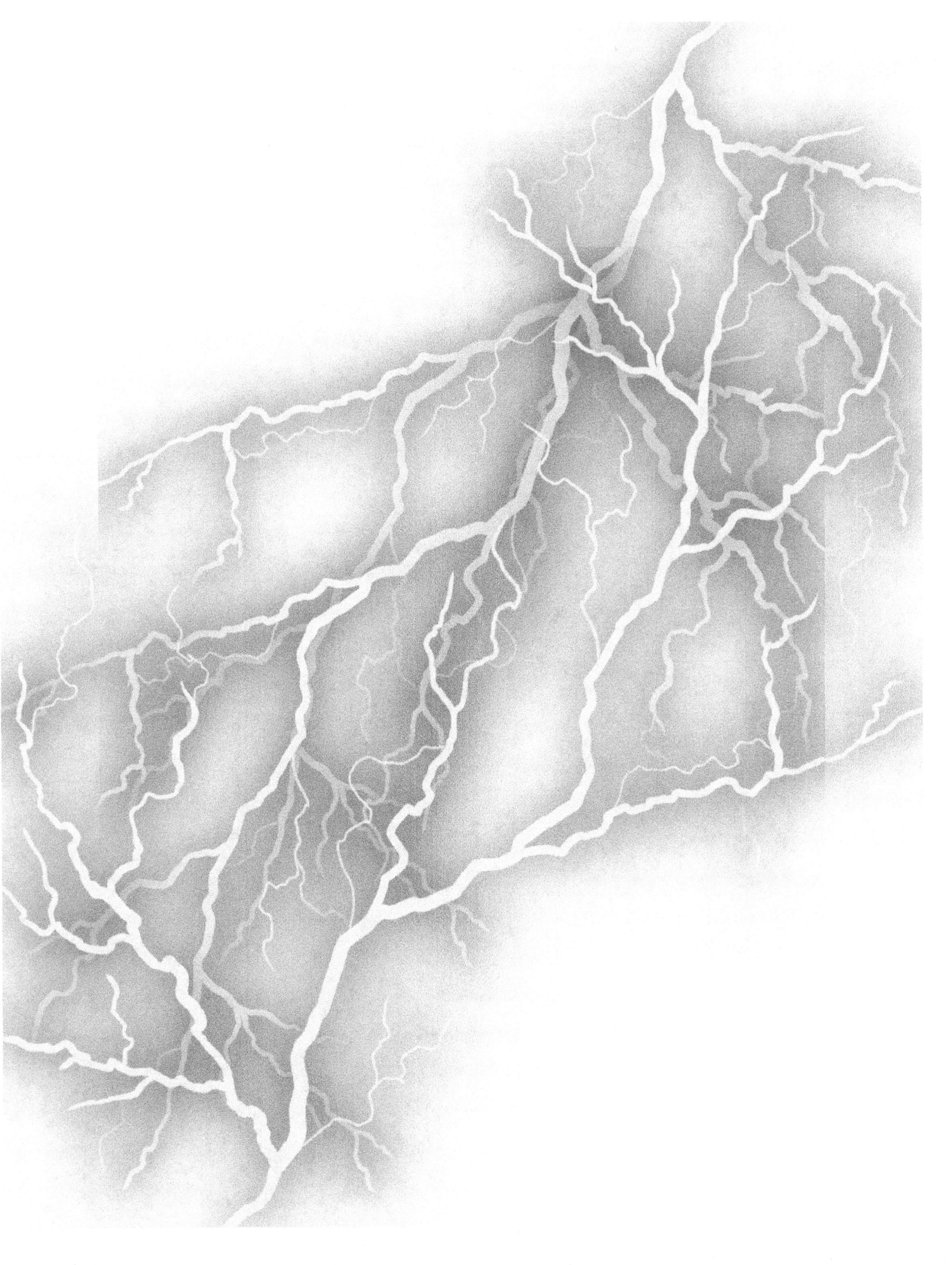

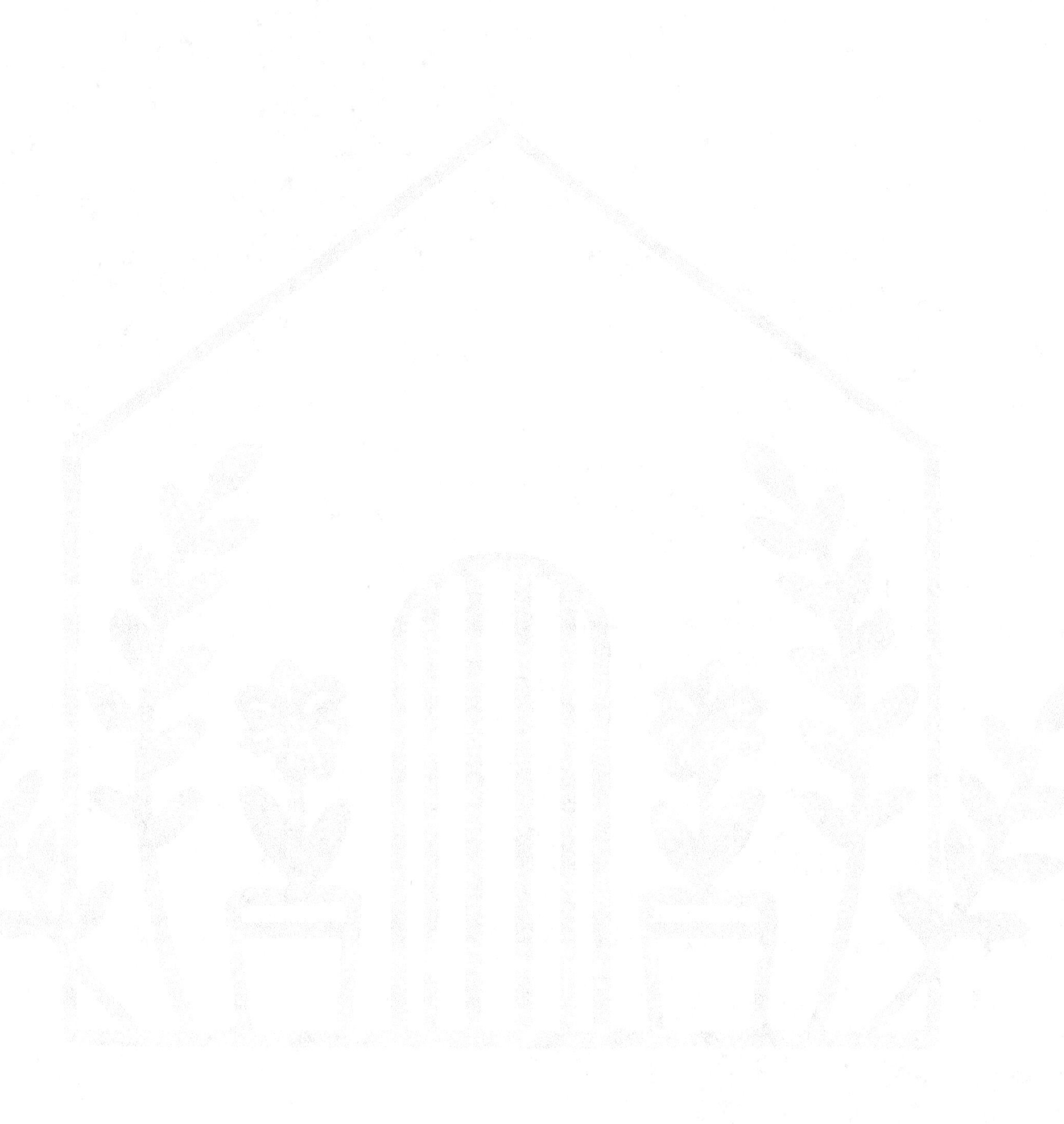

EMBARK ON A JOURNEY OF
RELAXATION AND CREATIVITY WITH
OUR ADULT GARDEN-THEMED COLORING
BOOK.
EXPLORE BEAUTIFULLY
CRAFTED ILLUSTRATIONS INSPIRED BY
THE WORLD OF GARDENING, FEATURING
INTRICATE
DESIGNS OF PLANTS, LEAVES, AND
IMAGINATIVE SYMBOLS.
IMMERSE YOURSELF IN
A CALMING AND VIBRANT PALETTE AS
YOU BRING TO LIFE SCENES
DEPICTING VARIOUS STRAINS
AND MOMENTS OF TRANQUILITY.
THIS ADULT COLORING BOOK OFFERS A
UNIQUE BLEND OF ARTISTIC EXPRESSION
AND MINDFULNESS, INVITING
YOU TO UNWIND AND FIND
INSPIRATION IN THE SOOTHING
EMBRACE OF GARDEN CULTURE.

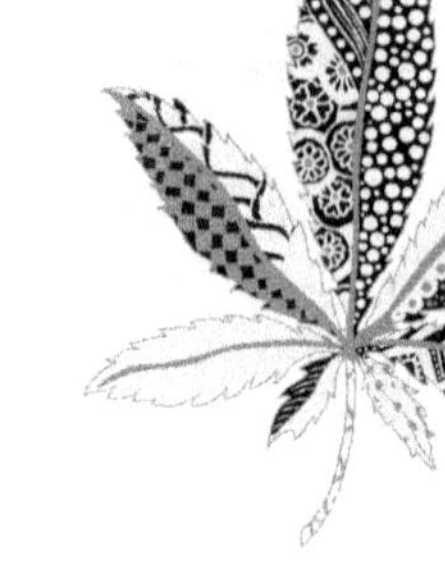